Third Edition

# FLUENCY

## Strategies & Assessments

Jerry L. Johns
Roberta L. Berglund

INTERNATIONAL
**Reading Association**
800 BARKSDALE ROAD, PO BOX 8139
NEWARK, DE 19714-8139, USA (302) 731-1600
www.reading.org

**KENDALL/HUNT PUBLISHING COMPANY**
4050 Westmark Drive Dubuque, Iowa 52002
www.kendallhunt.com/readingresources.html

## Book Team

Chairman and Chief Executive Officer: *Mark C. Falb*
Senior Vice President, College Division: *Thomas W. Gantz*
Director of National Book Program: *Paul B. Carty*
Editorial Development Manager: *Georgia Botsford*
Vice President, Production and Manufacturing: *Alfred C. Grisanti*
Assistant Vice President, Production Services: *Christine E. O'Brien*
Project Coordinator: *Angela Puls*
Cover Designer: *Jenifer Chapman*

## Author Information for Correspondence and Workshops

Jerry L. Johns, Ph.D.
Consultant in Reading
E-mail: *jjohns@niu.edu*
Fax: 815-899-3022

Roberta L. Berglund, Ed.D.
Consultant in Reading/Language Arts
E-mail: *bberglund@rocketmail.com*

## Ordering Information

Address:        Kendall/Hunt Publishing Company
                4050 Westmark Drive
                Dubuque, IA 52002
Telephone:      800-247-3458, ext. 4 or 5
Web site:       www.kendallhunt.com
Fax:            800-772-9165

1/31/07

# Contents

# Part 3: Passages and Resources for Fluency Checks     119

# Enter Here: A Quick Orientation to *Fluency*

**Are you wondering how to incorporate fluency strategies in your daily lessons?**

**Are you pressed for preparation time?**

**Do you have so many critical tasks to accomplish with your students that you simply can't find time to try one more thing?**

Help is on the way. We have written this easy to use resource with you, the educator, in mind. Our goal is to help you include fluency strategies in your instructional repertoire without adding hours of preparation time.

Most teachers, specialists, and reading coaches know that fluency is now accepted as a core component of a quality reading program. Fluency is also a critical component in programs designed for readers who struggle. The report of the National Reading Panel (2000) as well as recent articles (Hudson, Lane, & Pullen, 2005; Pikulski & Chard (2005) and books (e.g., Gunning, 2005; Rasinski, Blachowicz, & Lems, 2006; Vacca, Vacca, Gove, Burkey, Lenhart, & McKeon, 2006) highlight the importance of fluency.

We wrote *Fluency* for classroom teachers, prospective teachers, reading specialists and coaches, and other professionals involved in schools and educational agencies. This compact, focused book helps you understand fluency, offers many strategies to strengthen fluency instruction for students in regular classrooms as well as in resource rooms, and provides assessment strategies to help monitor students' progress.

## Part 1: Questions and Answers about Fluency

Part 1 presents a series of questions and answers about fluency. Here you will find helpful and concise answers to common questions teachers have asked about fluency. We suggest you begin with the Anticipation Guide (page 2) to help activate your background knowledge and ideas about fluency. Next, preview the questions and explore those that relate to your needs and interests. (Note: Answers to questions posed in the Anticipation Guide are provided in the Appendix.)

## Part 2: Evidence-Based Strategies, Activities, and Resources

Part 2 contains a wide range of evidence-based strategies, practical activities, and resources to develop students' fluency at various grade levels. The strategies selected were based on a review of the literature as well as helpful

**CLASSROOM PRACTICES
FOR FLUENCY**

Building Blocks

Shared Reading

Assisted Reading

Performance Reading

Independent Reading

Integrated Strategies

**Figure 1**

ideas shared by teachers. The strategies are arranged in six areas of classroom practice. See Figure 1.

**Building blocks for fluency** contains five important and general foundations for fluency including tips and suggestions for each area.

The remaining five areas—**shared reading, assisted reading, performance reading, independent reading,** and **integrated strategies** all have strategies arranged in a similar format:

Fluency goals (see the **bold** words around the fluency diamond)
Strategy name
Materials needed
Use (whole group, small group, partner, or individual)
Description
Step-by-step procedure for teaching the strategy
Evaluation (student behaviors to look for)

Take a look at Structured Repeated Reading on page 69 to see an example of the basic format. Note that the three **bold** words around the fluency diamond (accuracy, speed, expression) are the goals for the strategy. Reproducibles are included for many of the strategies.

We receive many positive comments from teachers regarding the organization of the various strategies. We invite your comments as well. Our contact information is given on the copyright page of this book.

## Part 3: Passages and Resources for Fluency Checks

Part 3 offers graded passages and related resources that help you assess students' growth in fluency. There are two sets of graded passages, narrative and informational, that range in difficulty from first through eighth grades.

You can have students read selected passages at various points in the school year to help monitor progress. There are reproducible record sheets for each passage. In addition, there are fluency record sheets, scales, and rubrics to record and monitor students' progress over time.

To summarize, we trust we have provided you with a solid base for understanding fluency by offering numerous ways to help students become confident readers who demonstrate greater fluency and by providing resources to document students' gains in fluency.

Jerry and Bobbi

# About the Authors

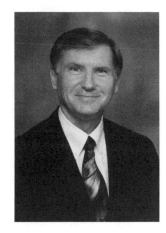

**Jerry L. Johns** has been recognized as a distinguished professor, writer, outstanding teacher educator, and popular speaker for schools, school districts, professional meetings, and Reading First conferences. His career was spent at Northern Illinois University along with visiting professorships at the University of Victoria in British Columbia and Western Washington University. He has taught students from kindergarten through college.

Dr. Johns is a past president of the International Reading Association, Illinois Reading Council, College Reading Association, and Northern Illinois Reading Council. He has received recognition for outstanding service to each of these professional organizations and is a member of the Illinois Reading Council Hall of Fame. Dr. Johns has served on numerous committees of the International Reading Association (IRA) and was a member of the Board of Directors. He has also received the Outstanding Teacher Educator in Reading Award from the International Reading Association.

Dr. Johns has been invited to consult, conduct workshops, and make presentations for teachers and professional groups throughout the United States and in seven countries. He has also prepared nearly 300 publications that have been useful to a diverse group of educators. His *Basic Reading Inventory,* now in its ninth edition, is widely used in undergraduate and graduate classes, as well as by practicing teachers. Dr. Johns recently coauthored the fourth edition of *Improving Reading: Strategies and Resources,* the third edition of *Teaching Reading Pre-K–Grade 3,* and the second editions of *Improving Writing, Strategies for Content Area Learning: Vocabulary, Comprehension, and Response,* and *Visualization: Using Mental Images to Strengthen Comprehension.*

**Roberta L. (Bobbi) Berglund** has had a long and distinguished career in education. Her public school experience spans more than twenty years and includes serving as a classroom teacher, reading specialist, Title I Director, and district curriculum administrator. Dr. Berglund has been a member of the reading faculty at the University of Wisconsin-Whitewater and has also taught graduate reading courses at Northern Illinois University, Rockford College, National-Louis University, and Aurora University. Currently Dr. Berglund is a consultant in the area of reading and language arts, working with school districts and regional offices of education in developing curriculum and assessments, conducting professional development, and guiding the selection of instructional materials for reading, spelling, writing, and related areas.

Dr. Berglund has received honors for outstanding service to several organizations and has been selected as a member of the Illinois Reading Council Hall of Fame. She also was honored with the Those Who Excel Award from the Illinois State Board of Education.

Dr. Berglund has served on several committees of the International Reading Association, including the program committees for the Annual

Convention and the World Congress. She has also chaired the Publications Committee.

Dr. Berglund has conducted numerous workshops for teachers and has been invited to make presentations at state, national, and international conferences. She is the author of over fifty publications and is the coauthor of several professional books, including *Strategies for Content Area Learning: Vocabulary, Comprehension, and Response,* and *Comprehension and Vocabulary Strategies for the Elementary Grades.*

# Part 1

# Questions and Answers about Fluency

# Overview & Anticipation Guide

This part of the book provides a series of questions and answers related to fluency. We have also provided an anticipation guide so you can react to some statements about fluency before you read the questions and answers.

## Anticipation Guide for Fluency

### ⟨XX⟩ Directions ▶◆◆

Before reading the questions and answers, read the statements below and check those with which you agree. Note: the answers are provided in the appendix.

**BEFORE READING**

| Agree | Disagree | |
|---|---|---|
| _____ | _____ | 1. Fluency in reading is most relevant at the beginning stages of reading. |
| _____ | _____ | 2. Fluency is independent of comprehension. |
| _____ | _____ | 3. Research has identified several methods to increase reading fluency. |
| _____ | _____ | 4. Oral reading fluency is developed best through independent reading. |
| _____ | _____ | 5. One aspect of fluency can be judged by determining the student's rate of reading in words per minute (WPM). |
| _____ | _____ | 6. It is appropriate to consider fluency in silent reading. |
| _____ | _____ | 7. Fluency is actually speed of reading. |
| _____ | _____ | 8. Fluency strategies are primarily for students experiencing difficulty in reading. |
| _____ | _____ | 9. Students should adjust reading rate according to their purposes for reading. |
| _____ | _____ | 10. A reasonable oral fluency rate for third-grade students is 160 words correct per minute (WCPM) by the end of the school year. |
| _____ | _____ | 11. Round-robin oral reading is an effective fluency activity. |

# 1. What Is Fluency?

Reading fluency is the ability to read with comprehension, accuracy, speed, and expression. Fluency has been identified as a "very hot" topic for 2006 (Cassidy & Cassidy (2005/2006). According to the National Reading Panel (2000), fluency is reading text "with speed, accuracy, and proper expression." It is an essential element of reading instruction. Over the last two decades, the concept of fluency has been extended to include comprehension processes (Samuels, 2002). "After it is fully developed, reading fluency refers to a level of reading accuracy and rate where decoding is relatively effortless; where oral reading is smooth and accurate with correct prosody [expression]; and where attention can be allocated to comprehension" (Wolf & Katzir-Cohen, 2001, p. 219).

**Figure 1.1**
The Components
of Fluency

Although fluency pertains to both oral and silent reading, fluency is often associated with oral reading, because teachers can observe accuracy by recording the number of miscues the student makes while reading and can also note the student's rate, phrasing, and expression. Generally, it is assumed that oral reading is similar, but not identical, to students' silent reading. Speed and comprehension can be evaluated in both oral and silent reading. You might find it useful to think of fluency as having four components: 1) speed, 2) accuracy, 3) appropriate expression, and 4) comprehension. See Figure 1.1.

**Comprehension** refers to understanding. Without comprehension, reading is merely word calling or barking at print. Comprehension is usually evaluated through retellings, answering questions, discussions, drawing/art, dramatic interpretation, or some combination of these methods. Fluency is related to reading comprehension, so helping students read quickly, accurately, and smoothly helps improve comprehension (Kuhn & Stahl, 2004; National Reading Panel, 2000; Pikulski; & Chard, 2005; Pinnell, Pikulski, Wixson, Campbell, Gough, & Beatty, 1995).

**Accuracy** means that the student recognizes most words automatically with little effort or attention (Samuels, 2002). It should be expected that students will make some miscues (for example, mispronouncing, omitting, or inserting words) during reading. If the student misses more than 10% of the words in a passage (one word in ten), the text or material is probably too difficult to use for instruction (Johns, 2005a).

**Speed** refers to rate of reading, usually determined in words per minute (WPM) or words correct per minute (WCPM). "A consensus exists among researchers that reading rate is a crucial factor in determining reading fluency at all levels" (Breznitz, 2006, p. 9). "WCPM has been shown . . . to serve as an accurate and powerful indicator of overall reading competence, especially in its strong correlation with comprehension" (Hasbrouck & Tindal, 2006, p. 636). In the answer to question 4, we will show you how to determine a student's reading speed or rate.

**Appropriate expression** means that the student uses phrasing, tone, and pitch so that oral reading sounds conversational. Prosody (prŏs′ ə-dē) is the term commonly used for these elements (Dowhower, 1991). Note the slashes in the following sentence; they provide an example of what proper expression would approximate when read aloud.

*The frisky dog/ ran quickly/ to the front door.*

## 2. Why Is Fluency Important?

In essence, students who are fluent readers are better able to devote their attention to comprehending the text. LaBerge and Samuels (1974) presented the basic theory underlying fluency. A student has only so much attention to focus on comprehension. As more and more of that attention is devoted to recognizing words, the result is likely to be limited reading fluency and comprehension. Fluency, then, generally results in increased comprehension.

There are other reasons why fluency is important. Students in elementary, middle, and high school who experience difficulty in reading, for the most part, lack fluency. To help students who struggle in reading, attention in the instructional program should be devoted to fluency. "It is generally acknowledged that fluency is a critical component of skilled reading" (National Reading Panel, 2000, p. 3-1). For example, Shanahan (2000a), in his framework for literacy instruction, identifies fluency as one of the major components. Heilman, Blair, and Rupley (2002) also identify fluency as a major instructional task. Fluency with text also helps to affirm and support the student's positive perception as a reader.

## 3. Does Fluency Apply to Silent Reading?

Yes. As discussed earlier, fluency is often thought about in relation to oral reading; nevertheless, fluency is also important in silent reading if students are to be efficient and effective readers. Silent reading also becomes more important as students move through the grades. Ultimately, most of the reading done by students and adults is silent reading. Because silent reading is used so commonly, the rate at which students comprehend is an important instructional consideration.

Carver (1989) has provided some helpful information on silent reading rates. The figures he provides are the average reading rates of students in a particular grade who can understand material at that grade level. Note that rate is considered in tandem with comprehension or understanding. Carver presents his rate figures in standard word lengths, but you can determine a student's rate (which we answer in the next question) and compare it to the figures in Table 1. Such a comparison will give you an indication of how the student's rate compares with the rates at which average students in a particular grade read with understanding.

**TABLE 1**

Silent Reading Rates for Students in Various Grades Who Understand the Material

| GRADE | WPM |
|-------|---------|
| 1 | <81 |
| 2 | 82–108 |
| 3 | 109–130 |
| 4 | 131–147 |
| 5 | 148–161 |
| 6 | 162–174 |
| 7 | 175–185 |
| 8 | 186–197 |
| 9 | 198–209 |
| 10 | 210–224 |
| 11 | 225–240 |
| 12 | 241–255 |

# 4. How Is Rate of Reading Determined?

Reading rate is often reported in words per minute (WPM). The same procedure can be used for oral and silent reading. Basically, the procedure involves having the student read a selection while you time the reading, using a stopwatch or a watch with a second hand. The following steps will permit you to determine a student's rate of reading in WPM. See example in Figure 1.2.

1. Count or estimate the number of words in the selection. If the passage is short (175 words or less), actually count the words. If the passage is longer, you can estimate the number of words by counting the number of words on a representative line of text and counting the number of lines. Then you multiply the two numbers to get an estimate of the number of words in the passage. For example, if there are 30 lines in the passage, with 10 words on a representative line, there would be approximately 300 words (30 × 10 = 300) in the passage.

2. Multiply by 60 (300 × 60 = 18000). This step is necessary to determine WPM.

3. This numeral becomes the dividend (18000).

4. Time the student's reading in seconds (e.g., 90 seconds).

5. This numeral becomes the divisor (90).

6. Do the necessary division. The resulting numeral is the quotient, which is words per minute (WPM).

If the resulting numeral is based on silent reading, use Table 1 from question 3. If the student reads orally, use Table 2 presented in the answer to the next question.

You will notice that Table 2 uses words **correct** per minute (WCPM) in reporting oral reading rates. To determine WCPM, follow the same six steps outlined in question 3. Once your determine WPM, total and subtract the number of mispronunciations, substitutions, omissions, reversals, and pauses on words for at least three seconds (pronounce the word for the student after three seconds). The result will be WCPM. For example, if a student achieves a rate of 137 WPM but makes two mispronunciations, one substitution, and two omissions, there are five miscues. You merely subtract these five miscues from 137. The result is 132 WCPM.

## 5. What Oral Reading Rates Are Appropriate for Different Grade Levels?

The answer to this straightforward question is more complex than it appears. One reason for this complexity is that there is no consensus in the literature (Bear & Barone, 1998; Rasinski & Padak, 1996). Another reason is that classrooms and schools can differ in many variables that impact so-called average oral reading rates. Perhaps the best advice is to develop local rates for different grade levels. Such advice, however, means more work for

Example
1. 300
2. 18000
3. )18000
4. 90
5. 90 )18000

     200 WPM
6. 90 )18000
     180

**Figure 1.2**

**TABLE 2**  Oral Reading Norms for Students in Grades One through Eight

| GRADE (N) | PERCENTILE | FALL | | WINTER | | SPRING | |
|---|---|---|---|---|---|---|---|
| | | N | WCPM | N | WCPM | N | WCPM |
| 1 (74,623) | 90 | | 32 | | 75 | | 105 |
| | 75 | | 14 | | 43 | | 78 |
| | 50 | 2,847 | 7 | 33,366 | 22 | 38,410 | 50 |
| | 25 | | 2 | | 11 | | 27 |
| | 10 | | 1 | | 6 | | 14 |
| 2 (99,699) | 90 | | 102 | | 124 | | 141 |
| | 75 | | 77 | | 99 | | 116 |
| | 50 | 29,634 | 50 | 33,683 | 72 | 36,382 | 89 |
| | 25 | | 24 | | 44 | | 62 |
| | 10 | | 12 | | 19 | | 34 |
| 3 (96,460) | 90 | | 128 | | 145 | | 161 |
| | 75 | | 100 | | 119 | | 137 |
| | 50 | 29,832 | 72 | 32,371 | 91 | 34,257 | 107 |
| | 25 | | 46 | | 60 | | 78 |
| | 10 | | 24 | | 36 | | 47 |
| 4 (87,436) | 90 | | 144 | | 165 | | 180 |
| | 75 | | 119 | | 139 | | 152 |
| | 50 | 29,609 | 94 | 27,373 | 111 | 30,454 | 124 |
| | 25 | | 69 | | 86 | | 99 |
| | 10 | | 42 | | 60 | | 72 |
| 5 (82,073) | 90 | | 165 | | 181 | | 194 |
| | 75 | | 137 | | 155 | | 167 |
| | 50 | 28,510 | 109 | 25,229 | 126 | 28,334 | 138 |
| | 25 | | 85 | | 98 | | 108 |
| | 10 | | 60 | | 73 | | 81 |
| 6 (57,575) | 90 | | 177 | | 194 | | 204 |
| | 75 | | 153 | | 166 | | 178 |
| | 50 | 18,923 | 127 | 17,668 | 140 | 20,984 | 150 |
| | 25 | | 98 | | 111 | | 122 |
| | 10 | | 67 | | 81 | | 93 |
| 7 (29,135) | 90 | | 176 | | 188 | | 200 |
| | 75 | | 154 | | 162 | | 176 |
| | 50 | 10,687 | 127 | 7,313 | 134 | 11,135 | 150 |
| | 25 | | 102 | | 108 | | 122 |
| | 10 | | 79 | | 86 | | 97 |
| 8 (24,105) | 90 | | 183 | | 193 | | 198 |
| | 75 | | 160 | | 168 | | 176 |
| | 50 | 8,674 | 130 | 5,986 | 142 | 9,445 | 151 |
| | 25 | | 104 | | 112 | | 124 |
| | 10 | | 79 | | 84 | | 97 |

N: Number of student scores
WCPM: Words correct per minute

school personnel. The results of such efforts, if undertaken in a thoughtful and consistent manner, will provide meaningful and useful data. To help teachers who may not have the time or desire to establish local norms for oral reading rates, we provide norms for grades one through eight.

Norms provided by Johns (2005b) were updated (see Table 2) using four sources of information. The first was a five-year study by Forman and Sanders (1998) which established norms for first-grade students. Over 3,500 scores were obtained from students who took part in their study. These students were from a large suburban school district whose students score considerably above average on state and national reading assessments. Norms were provided for three points of the school year.

The second source was a study by Hasbrouck and Tindal (1992). Their study involved over 7,000 scores from students in grades two through five who read passages at sight for one minute from their grade-level texts, regardless of the students' instructional levels. Because most classrooms have students who represent a wide range of reading levels, their procedure resulted in some students reading passages that were presumed to be easy (independent level), while other students were asked to read passages that would be too difficult (frustration level). The norms provide words correct per minute at the 75th, 50th, and 25th percentiles for students in grades two through five at three points (fall, winter, and spring) in the school year.

The third source of reading fluency data was gathered beginning in 1999 and ending with the 2002–2003 school year (www.edformation.com). Over 240,000 scores for students in grades one through eight who read passages for one minute were analyzed. The passages were at grade level, which meant that they were easy for some students and difficult for other students. Separate norms were calculated for each of the four school years. The resulting norms for each year provide words correct per minute at the 90th, 75th, 50th, 25th, and 10th percentiles at three points (fall, winter, and spring) of the school year.

The fourth source of data was a follow-up study by Hasbrouck and Tindal (2006) using over 297,000 scores obtained from students in grades one through eight. Students represented all achievement levels, including those identified as gifted or reading disabled. English Language Learners (ELLs) who were receiving reading instruction in a regular classroom were also included in the data. Schools and districts from 23 states used curriculum based measures (CBMs) for the assessment. This procedure resulted in some students reading materials at their frustration levels. Norms were compiled for students performing at the 90th, 75th, 50th, 25th, and 10th percentiles at three points throughout the school year, fall, winter, and spring, with the exception of grade one (which reported students' fluency norms for only the winter and spring).

All these data were thoughtfully studied, analyzed, and compiled using professional judgment (see Table 2). The resulting table is intended to provide helpful information to teachers who desire to have some guidelines for students' reading rates. Because the norms are in words correct per minute (WCPM), comparing them to words per minute (WPM), as suggested in this book, means that there is a slightly different basis for comparison. Comparisons can still be done and subsequently used to make informal

**TABLE 3**  Mean Words Correct Per Minute "Targets"*
for Average Students in Grades One through Eight

| GRADE | FALL "TARGET" | WINTER "TARGET" | SPRING "TARGET" |
|:---:|:---:|:---:|:---:|
| 1 | Not Applicable | 20 | 50 |
| 2 | 50 | 70 | 90 |
| 3 | 70 | 90 | 110 |
| 4 | 95 | 110 | 125 |
| 5 | 110 | 125 | 140 |
| 6 | 125 | 140 | 150 |
| 7 | 125 | 140 | 150 |
| 8 | 130 | 140 | 150 |

*"Targets" are reported in round numbers.

appraisals regarding students' rates of reading. Remember that the rates in Table 2 are more conservative than the rates determined by the WPM method. The percentiles within each grade level can be used informally to help you track and monitor student progress in rate within a particular grade throughout the school year.

In recent years, there has been mention of desired reading rates for various instructional levels or rate "targets" for average students in various grades. Using the three sources of information previously described, Table 3 was developed. A recent technical report (Behavioral Research and Teaching, 2005) reported very similar findings at the 50th percentiles for the same grade levels. This table provides rate "targets" for average students at three points in the school year. These numbers are less than the "challenging" rates created by Carnine, Silbert, Kame'enui, and Tarver (2004, pp. 192–193) based on students who were performing very well on standardized tests. They argue that helping students achieve high rates of fluency in the early grades leads to more reading by the student and makes school a more enjoyable experience. Keep in mind that the "targets" are best used informally to determine students' progress in comparison with the so-called average students. Based on the data for grade six and beyond, the target rate for the spring of the year levels at 150 words correct per minute. Because of individual differences in student ability and learning rates, expecting all students to reach the target is unrealistic.

## 6. How Should the Norms for Oral Reading Be Used?

The information in Table 2 can provide one basis for judging students' rates, but there are several important points to keep in mind when using the oral reading norms provided in this book or from other sources.

First, and most important, oral reading rates should not be considered synonymous with fluency. Rate is *one* of the four components of fluency; the other three are accuracy, expression, and comprehension. Failure to take each of these components into account can lead to distortions of a more complete construct of fluency (Rasinski, 2006). For example, a student who has a high reading rate with minimal comprehension will need a different sort of instruction than a student with a slow reading rate who has excellent comprehension. Even a student who reads orally very quickly with good comprehension may need some instruction on expressive oral reading, perhaps using strategies like Guess the Emotion (page 92), Say it Like the Character (page 90), and Super Signals (page 50).

Second, there are several important variables that can impact fluency—such as the type of text. Texts can be broadly characterized as narrative and informational. It is likely that a student will have more fluent reading with a story than with a selection from informational text (e.g., science and social studies). The student's purpose for reading may also impact fluency. The common one-minute reads used by many schools to determine rate may predispose some students to get through the passage quickly without a concern for accuracy, expression, and/or comprehension. Prior knowledge is another variable that influences fluency. The student who possesses an extensive amount of knowledge about a particular topic will likely have an advantage over the student whose background knowledge is severely limited. Unfortunately, fluency norms give no attention to these important variables, so it is up to you to be mindful of them when assessing oral reading rate and using fluency norms.

Finally, it is vital to recognize that an instructional program should be based on a deep construct of fluency. Pikulski and Chard (2005) identify nine areas that should be included in such a program. Our adaptation of their ideas follows: 1) graphophonic (phonics, phonemic awareness) foundations; 2) building sight vocabulary and building oral language skills; 3) providing instruction in the acquisition of a basic sight vocabulary; 4) teaching common words and spelling patterns; 5) teaching, modeling, and providing practice in helpful decoding strategies; 6) using appropriate instructional level texts to teach fluency; 7) using repeated reading procedures (Echo Reading, Readers Theater, Structured Repeated Reading, etc.), especially for readers who struggle; 8) encouraging wide independent reading (Read and Relax, Sustained Silent Reading); and 9) using appropriate assessment procedures to monitor fluency development (narrative and informational passages). Chart 1 on the next page identifies strategies in *Fluency* for each of these areas.

## 7. What Are Some Ways to Assess Fluency?

Various assessment perspectives have been offered by the contributors to *What Research Has to Say About Reading Instruction* (Samuels & Farstrup, 2006). We suggest a combination of quantitative (numbers) and qualitative (behaviors) criteria. There are often numbers related to reading rate

## Building Fluency into the Instructional Program

| ELEMENTS OF THE INSTRUCTIONAL PROGRAM INCORPORATING FLUENCY (Pikulski & Chard, 2005) | FLUENCY: STRATEGIES & ASSESSMENTS (Johns & Berglund, 2006) |
|---|---|
| Graphophonic (phonics, phonemic awareness) | Phonemic Awareness (pages 30–31) Phonics Instruction and Practice (pages 36–37) Context Instruction and Practice (page 39–40) |
| Building Sight Vocabulary and Oral Language Skills | Word Identification (pages 36–40) Basic Sight Vocabulary (pages 32–35) |
| Providing Instruction in Sight Vocabulary | Basic Sight Vocabulary (pages 32–35) |
| Teaching Common Words and Spelling Patterns | Word Identification (pages 36–40) |
| Teaching Decoding Strategies | Word Identification (pages 36–40) |
| Using Appropriate Instructional Level Text | Overview (page 22) |
| Using Repeated Reading Procedures | Structured Repeated Reading (pages 69–72) Simplified Repeated Reading (pages 73–74) Student Self-Managed Repeated Reading (pages 75–79) Tape, Check, Chart (pages 80–82) Klassroom Karaoke (pages 87–88) |
| Encouraging Wide Independent Reading | Read and Relax (pages 102–104) Sustained Silent Reading (pages 105–108) |
| Using Appropriate Assessment Practices | Passages and Resources for Fluency Checks (pages 119–163) |

**Chart 1**

expressed in words per minute (WPM). Tables 1 and 2 contain numbers that can be used in a quantitative manner. You can also keep track of how accurately a student reads by counting the number of miscues (e.g., mispronunciations, repetitions, insertions, substitutions, and omissions) made during the reading of a passage. The method of Structured Repeated Reading, described in Part 2 of this book, offers one way to help judge a student's progress as the same passage is reread over a period of days.

Examples of qualitative behaviors that can be noted are listed below.

✦ voice quality

✦ expression and emphasis

✦ phrasing and pauses

✦ appropriate use of punctuation

Some teachers develop an informal fluency rubric that can be used to judge qualitative aspects of fluency. We have provided two such rubrics in Part 3 that you may wish to use. One is a 4-Point Fluency Rubric for Oral Reading. The other is used in the National Assessment of Educational Progress (NAEP's Holistic Oral Reading Fluency Scale). Part 3 of this book also contains some graded passages that can be used for fluency checks. These passages range in difficulty from first grade through eighth grade. Use these fluency checks with individual students or as part of the Classroom Fluency Snapshot in Figure 1.3. These passages also have provisions for you to evaluate comprehension and expression.

The Classroom Fluency Snapshot (CFS), developed by Blachowicz, Sullivan, and Cieply (2001), offers another way to assess fluency. This assessment shows clearly how a student's reading rate compares with others in the classroom. The CFS can be used in the fall of the school year to help establish baseline data for the class. Subsequent snapshots can be used throughout the year to measure and monitor student progress. The chart in the sidebar to the left shows an example from a second-grade classroom. Charts for your use can be found in the Resources for Part 3. Below is an adapted step-by-step procedure for using the CFS with a class of students.

1. Select a passage that is representative of the material you will use for instruction or use one of the passages provided in Part 3. All students will read the same passage, so make sufficient teacher copies for your use. The majority of students should be able to read the passage with at least 85% to 90% initial accuracy. Choose a passage that will take students one or two minutes to read. Although the passage will be difficult for some of your poorer readers, you will be able to establish baseline data for the entire class.

**Materials Needed**

✦ the copy of the passage for the student to read.

✦ a copy of the passage on which you will mark miscues (any deviation from what's written) such as omissions, insertions, mispronunciations, ignoring or adding punctuation, and words pronounced

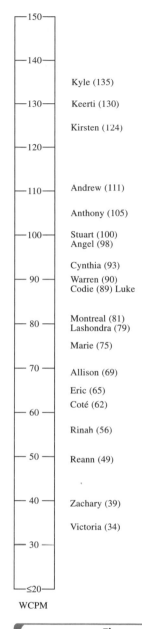

**Figure 1.3**
Classroom Fluency Snapshot

after waiting three seconds. You may mark the actual miscues where they occur in the text if you are familiar with coding miscues or use a running record procedure. If you are not experienced with coding miscues, merely make a check mark over each miscue. A method for coding miscues can be found in Johns (2005a).

◇ a stopwatch or a watch with a second hand to time the student's reading.

◇ a tape recorder if you wish to do the analysis later or recheck your coding of miscues and the number of seconds taken for reading.

2. Invite individual students to read the passage to you. You could offer an introductory statement like: "Please read this passage about _____ at a speed that's just right for you. Read as accurately as you can. When you have finished reading, I'll ask you a few questions (or I'll ask you to retell what you have read)." At the end of one minute, make a mark after the last word read by the student. Invite a short retelling or ask some questions based on the selection.

3. Count the number of words read in one minute and then subtract the number of miscues (e.g., mispronunciations, substitutions, omissions, reversals, and ignored punctuation). An easy way to determine word counts is to place a numeral at the end of each line to indicate the cumulative number of words. Use this information to quickly determine the number of words the student read and then subtract the number of miscues to determine words correct per minute. A partial sample is shown in Figure 1.4.

4. Compile the results for all the students on a sample chart like that shown in Figure 1.3 to see the range of rates in your class and to help determine which students might profit from instruction to increase

---

**At the Farm**

$\overset{about}{\underset{\lor}{\phantom{x}}}$     $\overset{wanted}{\phantom{x}}$

Sue was visiting her grandparents' farm for a week. She decided to have a picnic    15

in the woods. She packed a lunch with a peanut-butter and jelly sandwich, an apple,    31

The
When she remembered│Jane. She ran back to the house and got Jane, her favorite doll.    108

           *end of*
           *one minute*

Name __Stacy_____    Date ____9 – 29 –06_____

Total Words Read      __95__    Additional Notes/Comments: *good phrasing*

Number of Miscues      __3__

Words Correct per Minute      __92__

**Figure 1.4**

fluency. Repeating the process several times during the school year (see Figure 1.5) with the same or different passages should enable you to assess individual and class progress. There are two blank charts provided for your use in the Resources for Part 3. One chart is for the primary grades; the other chart is for the upper grades. They can be used to chart classroom data in a manner similar to that on page 14.

## 8.  What's Wrong with Round-Robin Oral Reading?

Round robin oral reading is "the outmoded practice of calling on students to read orally one after the other" (Harris & Hodges, 1995, p. 222). It often refers to oral reading done at sight in the context of whole class or small group instruction and looks something like this: "Class, turn to page 53 in your books. José, you begin reading. I want the rest of the class to follow along." As José reads, some students are reading ahead, some are actually following along, and others are looking out the window or daydreaming. You may even recall some of your own experiences with round-robin oral reading. Rarely are positive comments shared about the practice (Johns & Galen, 1977).

Round-robin oral reading rarely fulfills the purposes of oral reading.

So what's wrong with round-robin oral reading? Ash and Kuhn (2006) note that "it runs counter to research on good literacy instruction" (p. 156). Here's our list of common objections to the practice:

- ✧ It focuses mostly on oral reading performance, rather than understanding.
- ✧ It rarely engages students (except the student who is reading).
- ✧ It has little connection to reading in real life.
- ✧ It reduces the time that could be better spent on quality instructional practices.
- ✧ It teaches students very little.
- ✧ It is embarrassing to poorer readers.

According to Hyatt (1943), who traced the history and development of oral reading over a sixty-year period, oral reading is worthwhile only when it 1) informs or entertains an audience; 2) enables students to participate in a group activity (such as choral reading); or 3) increases one's personal pleasure by reading aloud beautiful passages of literature. Unfortunately, round-robin oral reading rarely, if ever, fulfills any of these three purposes.

When it comes to fluency, there is no doubt that *meaningful oral reading is important.* A study by Eldredge, Reutzel, and Hollingsworth (1996) found that round-robin oral reading was inferior to the shared book experience in reducing students' miscues, improving reading fluency, increasing vocabulary acquisition, and improving reading comprehension. In Part 2 of this book, we offer a number of oral reading practices that promote fluency without the negatives generally associated with round-robin oral reading.

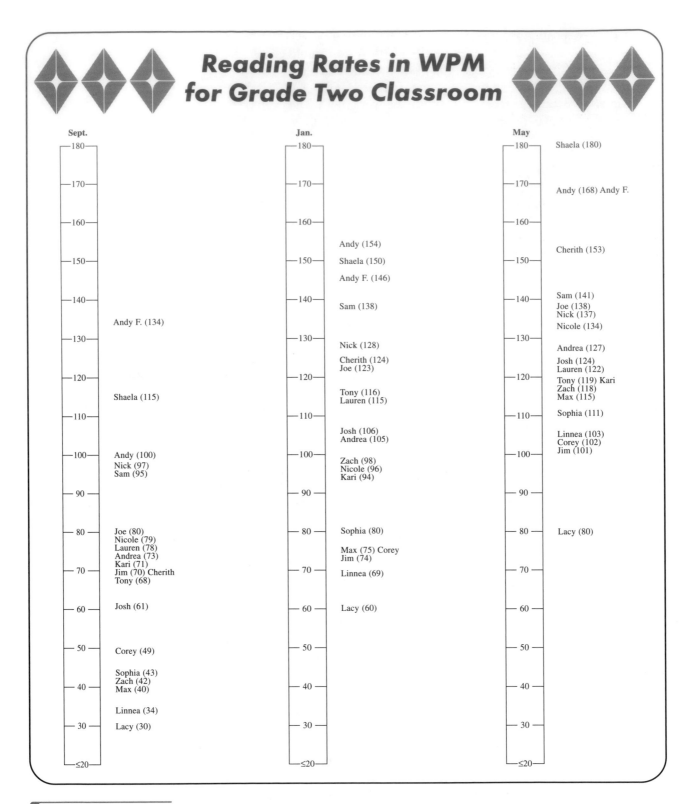

# Reading Rates in WPM for Grade Two Classroom

**Sept.**

- 180
- 170
- 160
- 150
- 140
- 130 — Andy F. (134)
- 120 — Shaela (115)
- 110
- 100 — Andy (100) / Nick (97) / Sam (95)
- 90
- 80 — Joe (80) / Nicole (79) / Lauren (78) / Andrea (73) / Kari (71)
- 70 — Jim (70) Cherith / Tony (68)
- 60 — Josh (61)
- 50 — Corey (49)
- 40 — Sophia (43) / Zach (42) / Max (40)
- Linnea (34)
- 30 — Lacy (30)
- ≤20

**Jan.**

- 180
- 170
- 160
- 150 — Andy (154) / Shaela (150) / Andy F. (146)
- 140 — Sam (138)
- 130 — Nick (128) / Cherith (124) / Joe (123)
- 120 — Tony (116) / Lauren (115)
- 110 — Josh (106) / Andrea (105)
- 100 — Zach (98) / Nicole (96) / Kari (94)
- 90
- 80 — Sophia (80)
- Max (75) Corey / Jim (74)
- 70 — Linnea (69)
- 60 — Lacy (60)
- 50
- 40
- 30
- ≤20

**May**

- 180 — Shaela (180)
- 170 — Andy (168) Andy F.
- 160
- 150 — Cherith (153)
- 140 — Sam (141) / Joe (138) / Nick (137) / Nicole (134)
- 130 — Andrea (127) / Josh (124) / Lauren (122)
- 120 — Tony (119) Kari / Zach (118) / Max (115)
- 110 — Sophia (111)
- 100 — Linnea (103) / Corey (102) / Jim (101)
- 90
- 80 — Lacy (80)
- 70
- 60
- 50
- 40
- 30
- ≤20

**Figure 1.5**

# 9. What Part of the Reading Program Should Be Devoted to Fluency Instruction?

In the position statement of the International Reading Association (2000, p. 3), "the ability to read fluently" is among the skills students need to become readers. Shanahan (2000a) suggests that up to 25% of the instructional time for reading should be focused on fluency instruction. That percentage may be high, but it is clear that fluency is one aspect of the reading program that is often neglected (Allington, 1983a; Teale & Shanahan, 2001). The amount of time devoted to fluency instruction may depend on the grade level and the student's facility with word identification. It is important to consider the use of fluency strategies in each area of a balanced reading program: reading aloud, shared reading, guided reading, and independent reading. Most of the strategies in this book can be used in one or more of these areas. It is important to remember that fluency strategies can also be practiced and used in the content areas not only to improve fluency, but also to increase comprehension and the enjoyment of reading informational text.

> The ability to read fluently is among the skills students need to become readers.

In the primary literacy standards, fluency is a standard in kindergarten, first grade, and second grade (New Standards Primary Literacy Committee, 1999). Descriptions of fluency examples for each of these three grades follow.

Kindergarten—Shiori reads a 78-word book with adequate intonation. She pauses appropriately for periods at the end of each sentence and points to each word as she reads. "Although an adult reader might put more punctuation and drama into the reading to make it more interesting, Shiori's reading is considered fluent for the end of kindergarten" (New Standards Primary Literacy Committee, 1999, p. 59).

First Grade—Christopher reads a 279-word story fluently. "He could pause more appropriately at commas when they appear just before a quotation mark. Although he usually drops his voice to note the ends of sentences, the drop could be more emphatic" (New Standards Primary Literacy Committee, 1999, p. 100). Christopher's reading is basically fluent for the end of first grade because he sounds like he knows what he is reading.

Second Grade—Griffin reads a 631-word story "fluently as far as clear and correct pronunciation of words is concerned. His verbal emphasis on words and phrases signals the meaning of the text. However, his intonation and phrasing could be improved. He does not pause long enough within sections of dialogue to signal the end of the speaker's words. Sometimes he runs from one sentence right into another" (New Standards Literacy Committee, 1999, p. 147). Griffin's reading is considered fluent for the end of second grade.

As students move beyond second grade, they should continue to exhibit attention to punctuation, good intonation, appropriate phrasing, good voice quality, and dialogue. Because more and more of the students' reading will be done silently, these particular behaviors can be observed in contexts when oral reading is appropriate. Many of those contexts are presented in Part 2.

Fluency beyond the elementary grades has become a topic of interest in more recent years. One study (Rasinski, Padak, McKeon, Wilfong, Friedauer, & Heim, 2005) explored the decoding accuracy and reading rates of over 300 ninth graders in an urban high school. Students read a ninth-grade passage for one minute and then retold what they had read. The researchers found that students read with an average 97.4 percent in decoding accuracy and a reading rate of 136.4 words correct per minute. The average reading rate of these students was "below the 25th percentile *for eighth graders*" (p. 24). In addition, the reading fluency levels were correlated (r=.53) to students' comprehension performance. Although correlation does not imply causation, the findings led the researchers to conclude that reading fluency "needs to be considered even among high school students, and especially among struggling readers" (p. 25).

## 10.  What Insights Can Be Drawn from Research and Expert Opinion?

An analysis of the National Assessment of Educational Progress data revealed that approximately 44% of fourth grade students were unable to read grade-level material with adequate fluency (Pinnell, Pikulski, Wixson, Campbell, Gough, & Beatty, 1995). In recent years, there has been increased emphasis on research-based and evidenced-based practices related to reading. Kuhn and Stahl (2000) reviewed over forty studies related to fluency and concluded that "both assisted and unassisted methods of fluency instruction have been generally effective in facilitating rate and accuracy" (p. 25). Some of the studies also found improvements in students' comprehension.

After reviewing many studies, the contributors to the Report of the National Reading Panel (2000) noted that fluency can be improved for good readers as well as readers who struggle. "Classroom practices that encourage repeated oral reading with feedback and guidance lead to meaningful improvements in reading expertise for students" (National Reading Panel, 2000, p. 3-3). One way to judge the impact of guided oral reading procedures is to look at the effect size—the extent to which performance of the treatment group is greater than the performance of the control group. Effect sizes can be small (.20), moderate (.50), or large (.80). Table 4 shows the effect sizes for reading accuracy, fluency, and comprehension. "These data provide strong support for the supposition that instruction in guided oral reading is effective in improving reading" (National Reading Panel, 2000, p. 3-3).

Klenk and Kibby (2000) also reviewed fluency research. They found that repeated reading was a common method of developing fluency, especially

> Repeated oral reading with feedback and guidance leads to improvement in reading.

**TABLE 4** Effect Sizes of Repeated Oral Reading with Feedback on Three Reading Outcomes

| READING OUTCOME | EFFECT SIZE |
|---|---|
| Reading Accuracy | .55 |
| Reading Fluency | .44 |
| Reading Comprehension | .35 |

for students in the primary grades. They also noted that teacher modeling of the text students were about to read was another practice used to promote fluency. There are also many research studies (see Pearson & Fielding, 1991, for a review) that have shown relationships between the amount of reading students engage in and reading achievement. That finding suggests that recreational reading and other independent reading (like Sustained Silent Reading) in and out of school are important considerations in any efforts to increase fluency. Some specific procedures were also highlighted in the reviews of research (Repeated Reading, Neurological Impress, and Paired Reading), so we have included them in Part 2 of the book.

## 11. What Factors Can Impact Fluency?

The most fundamental and important basis for fluency is accuracy in word recognition. The significance of this area was pointed out by Anderson, Hiebert, Scott, and Wilkinson (1985), who noted that "one of the cornerstones of skilled reading is fast, accurate word identification." When the student recognizes most of the words quickly and easily, they are called sight words. The larger a student's sight vocabulary, the greater the likelihood that reading will be fluent. While automatic word recognition is necessary, it is not a sufficient indicator of fluent reading.

Other factors can also impact fluency:

The most important basis for fluency is accuracy in word recognition.

◇ Reading widely and often provides practice to solidify skills and helps promote confidence in reading.

◇ Opportunities to participate in meaningful activities for oral reading provide helpful models and practice.

◇ Listening to teachers read aloud on a daily basis provides an excellent model, enlarges students' vocabularies (Elley, 1988; Layne, 1996), and helps promote the value of reading.

There are also many direct and indirect actions you can take to teach and promote fluency. We present many of these actions, lessons, and tips in Part 2.

## 12. When Should Fluency Instruction Begin?

According to Kuhn and Stahl's review of research involving practices for developmental and remedial readers (2000), students need to have some basic reading ability before instruction focuses on fluency. Generally, this ability involves knowledge of sight vocabulary and an understanding of how print works. Students typically achieve this ability at the late pre-primer level. Older students who read at a late second-grade level or lower can also profit from fluency instruction. In addition, Worthy and Broaddus (2001/2002) note that fluency practice can also be used with older students to contribute to their comprehension and enjoyment of a wide range of textual materials. Although fluency instruction can generally begin in the second half of first grade, it is appropriate for students at any grade level who struggle with fluency.

## 13. What Are the Basic Principles of Fluency Instruction?

Our review of the research, extensive reading, and professional experience led to the formulation of the following set of foundational principles related to fluency instruction.

1. Fluency is one of three core elements of skilled reading; the other two are identifying words and constructing meaning. For students, fluency is the bridge or link between the ability to identify words quickly and the ability to understand text. It is an "important but often overlooked aspect of reading" (Strickland, Ganske, & Monroe, 2002, p. 120). If students read fluently, they can focus most of their attention on the meaningful and enjoyable aspects of reading (Burns, Griffin, & Snow, 1999). Figure 1.6 shows the role fluency plays in skilled reading.

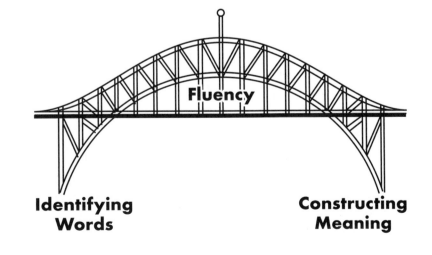

**Figure 1.6**

2.  Fluency is linked to comprehension. The impact of oral reading practice, feedback, and guidance on comprehension "is not inconsiderable, and in several comparisons it was actually quite high" (National Reading Panel, 2000, p. 3–18). Although there is reason to believe that oral reading practice and feedback have an impact on comprehension, we want to stress the importance of assessing comprehension or inviting retellings. Students need to understand that the goal of reading is the construction of meaning—not merely pronouncing words quickly and accurately. We want students to be meaning seekers who are able to read words quickly, easily, and meaningfully.

3.  Fluency develops from practice (National Reading Panel, 2000). A review of in-school voluntary reading programs (SSR, self-selected reading, and intensive reading) was conducted by Krashen (2004) to summarize the effects of such programs on tests of reading comprehension. He found that students in such programs did "as well or better than students who were engaged in traditional programs" (Krashen, 2004, p. 2). There is no substitute for an abundance of reading from a wide variety of printed materials. Commenting on independent reading, Samuels (2006) notes that "the amount of time spent in independent reading should match the student's reading ability. For higher ability readers, 40 minutes of independent reading proved to be effective. However, for the lower ability readers, 15 minutes of independent reading proved effective" (p. 33). In a recent study, Kuhn (2004/2005) combined practice with wide reading to significantly improve the comprehension of struggling readers. In Part 2 of the book, we offer a range of activities to help students practice reading. Some of the methods involve individual reading, partner reading, sharing in small groups, and whole class activities. A key feature of the practice is multiple readings of the same text. Such rereadings help build fluency and confidence.

> Students need to understand that the goal of reading is the construction of meaning.

4.  Fluency is dependent on a variety of factors. The difficulty, complexity, and interest level of the materials used for instruction and practice impact fluency. Ideally, materials should be appropriate in difficulty and of interest to students. Helpful sources of leveled books for use in kindergarten through sixth grade have been developed by Fountas and Pinnell (2000, 2001) and Pinnell and Fountas (2002).

5.  Fluency can be improved by teaching. Modeling, demonstrating, and thinking out loud are some of the explicit actions teachers can take to help students become fluent readers. You can model fluent reading and take time to discuss what makes reading fluent. Teaching phrasing and providing guided practice will also help remove some of the mystery of fluency. In short, be ready to be explicit with your instruction when it is necessary. Systematic teaching will not leave the skill of fluency to chance. In the words of Teale and Shanahan (2001, p. 8), "there are few positive changes as straightforward and potentially productive as an appropriate focus on fluency. It is time for us to stop ignoring the essential and to teach fluency as a regular part of our reading programs."

## 14. What Is the Purpose of Fluency Instruction?

A key feature of fluency practice is multiple readings of text.

The basic purpose of fluency instruction is to make it as easy as possible for students to comprehend text. Word-by-word reading, poor phrasing, and lack of expression all diminish students' ability to understand text. While inefficiency in identifying words is the most important factor in fluency for students who struggle in reading (Torgesen, 2004), data from the National Assessment of Educational Progress revealed that a large percentage of fourth graders tested could read accurately but not fluently (Pinnell et al., 1995). Fluency, then, is not ensured if students can recognize words automatically. What is needed for many students is an intentional approach to fluency as a core element in the reading program. Part 2 of this book offers a number of strategies, activities, and resources that will help you provide high-quality fluency instruction.

# Part 2

# Evidence-Based Strategies, Activities, and Resources

**Figure 2.1**

# Overview

This part of the book contains instructional principles, strategies, activities, and resources to help students become fluent readers. We begin with four foundational principles to guide your teaching. See Figure 2.1.

## 1. Match Students' Reading Abilities to Appropriate Materials for Instruction

Topping (2006) identifies the management of text difficulty as an important predisposing factor facilitating the development of fluency. To help match students' reading levels to appropriate instructional materials, you might want to use an informal reading inventory like the *Basic Reading Inventory* (Johns, 2005a). Three reading levels can be determined: independent, instructional, and frustration. The independent level is characterized by excellent word recognition (99% accuracy), comprehension (90%), and fluency. This would be the level for independent reading and Read and Relax (see page 102).

The instructional level is where instruction is likely to be most effective. There is an appropriate match between a student's reading level and the materials used for instruction or practice. The instructional level is characterized by good word recognition (95% or better) and comprehension (75%). If guided reading is used, materials should be selected that are at his or her instructional level. Instruction in fluency is usually done with materials that are at or near the student's instructional level. According to Burns (2001), a critical foundation of guided reading is that students read materials at their respective instructional levels. But as Opitz and Ford (2001) point out, matching texts with students "is anything but simple. The interaction among texts, readers, and reading contexts is highly complex and involves a number of variable factors." It is clear, however, that students should spend the majority of time with reading materials at their instructional (just right) level. Allington (2006) believes that many students who exhibit dysfluent reading are products of poorly designed instructional environments. Their dysfluency is "a signal that they have been routinely given the wrong texts, texts that are too difficult" (p. 101). Your goal should be to help students read materials at their instructional levels.

In recent years, there has been a tendency to lower placement standards, such as 90% in word recognition. Gunning (2005), however, argues that "it is strongly advised that you stick with the 95 to 98 percent word recognition standard" (p. 30). He then cites several research studies and states that "students do best when they can read at least 95 to 98 percent of the words" (Gunning, 2005, p. 30). Students who are placed in instructional materials according to the higher standards have a higher success rate, spend more time on task, and have a more positive attitude toward reading (Enz, 1989).

The third reading level, frustration, is characterized by 90% word recognition and 50% comprehension. Materials at this level are not generally appropriate for instruction and should be avoided. Unfortunately, too many students are asked to read materials at their frustration level. When this situation occurs, students are likely to exhibit lack of expression in oral reading, lip movement in silent reading, finger pointing, and difficulty in pronouncing words. Teachers observe that students become more impatient, disturbing to the classroom, and reliant on directions from others.

## 2. Model Oral Reading

Daily oral reading to students should be an integral part of the instructional program. Many professionals agree that reading orally to students:

- ✧ stimulates language development.
- ✧ helps students move naturally into reading.
- ✧ shows that reading is pleasurable.
- ✧ demonstrates that print is meaningful.
- ✧ fosters an interest in printed materials.
- ✧ stimulates students to react to what is read.
- ✧ helps develop favorable attitudes toward reading.
- ✧ encourages students to listen actively.
- ✧ serves as a model.
- ✧ builds rapport.
- ✧ shares the joy of reading.
- ✧ helps enlarge vocabulary.

With respect to fluency, students will hear you share how oral reading should sound. Phrasing, emphasis, and tone are some of the aspects of fluency that can be modeled through regular periods of reading aloud.

## 3. Provide Guided Oral Reading Opportunities

There are a number of guided oral reading procedures (e.g., radio reading, paired reading) in which teachers are typically involved, especially as these procedures are initially introduced and modeled. The impact of such teaching, modeling, and feedback results in student learning. The National Reading Panel (2000) concluded that such procedures had a consistent and positive impact on word recognition, fluency, and comprehension for a wide range of readers over a wide range of levels (i.e., first grade through college). Later in Part 2, we provide a number of ways you can provide repeated oral reading opportunities for students to improve fluency and overall reading achievement.

## 4. Offer Daily Opportunities for Students to Read Easy Materials Independently

The amount of time students spend in silent reading in the average classroom is small. "An estimate of silent reading in the typical primary school class is 7 or 8 minutes per day, or less than 10% of the total time devoted to reading. By the middle grades, silent reading time may average 15 minutes per school day" (Anderson, Hiebert, Scott, & Wilkinson, 1985, p. 76).

The National Reading Panel (2000) considered "all formal efforts to increase the amounts of independent or recreational reading" by students. Such reading should typically involve materials that are easy for the student. Materials at the student's easy or independent level are read with a high degree of accuracy (98% or more) and excellent comprehension (Johns, 2005a).

One popular and widely used effort to promote independent reading is sustained silent reading (Hunt, 1970) described on page 105. Providing a daily period for students to read easy materials independently:

◇ helps establish the habit of reading.

◇ provides opportunities for practice.

◇ promotes a love of reading.

◇ communicates the importance of reading.

◇ familiarizes students with many types of reading materials.

◇ encourages the selection of appropriate reading materials.

◇ helps get reluctant readers into books.

◇ allows freedom for students to self-select reading materials.

◇ has a settling effect in the classroom.

◇ fosters engagement with printed materials.

While research reviewed by the National Reading Panel (2000) did not clearly and convincingly establish the impact of independent reading on overall reading achievement, the Panel concluded that independent reading might be beneficial. "There is an extensive amount of correlational data [hundreds of studies] linking amount of reading and reading achievement" (National Reading Panel, 2000). More recently, Krashen (2004) summarized the impact of in-school voluntary reading programs (SSR, intensive reading, and self-selected reading) on tests of reading comprehension. The original studies were conducted between 1948 and 2001. He found that that "in 51 out of 54 comparisons (94 percent), readers do as well or better than students who were engaged in traditional programs" (Krashen, 2004, p. 2). In our professional judgment, therefore, voluntary reading is worthwhile, even if much of the evidence is correlational. We would not want to see less voluntary reading in classrooms.

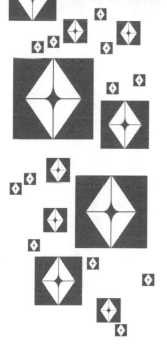

# Building Blocks for Fluency

# Teacher Read Alouds

**DESCRIPTION**

Being read to is widely considered to be a critical factor in becoming a successful reader (Routman, 2000). Reading aloud as little as fifteen minutes per day exposes children to the pleasure of reading and to a variety of books and genres. It also expands children's experiential base and develops positive attitudes towards reading in general. While reading aloud is sometimes considered most appropriate for primary-grade students, reading aloud is an excellent and appropriate activity for students of all ages. We believe that reading aloud to students is a critical building block for fluency. On the following page are suggested read alouds. Be sure to include selections from both narrative and informational sources in read-aloud experiences for your students. Before reading a book to students, read it yourself to confirm that it is appropriate and to check for elements that might challenge students' understanding. Reading aloud should be accompanied by prereading and postreading discussion (Gunning, 2000). For additional read-aloud suggestions, see Sullivan (2004) and the Indiana Library Federation (2001).

## Tips for Reading Aloud

1. Preview the selection before reading it aloud to students.

2. Introduce the read-aloud selection by displaying the text, discussing the title and author, and inviting students to make predictions about the selection's content.

3. During reading, hold the text so that students can see any illustrations. Use your voice to convey the emotions suggested by the text and to highlight any important information. Stop periodically to clarify any words or concepts that may be unfamiliar to students and encourage students to predict what will happen next. Also, invite students to comment on or make a personal connection to the text.

4. After reading, invite students to respond to the text, make connections to their own lives or to topics related to the classroom, and discuss how their predictions changed as they listened.

Following is a list of some favorite read-aloud books. While all are designated for a specific grade range, some of them may be used across several grade levels. For example, *Charlotte's Web* is a favorite for a wide range of ages, and *The Tale of Despereaux* is enjoyed by primary-grade as well as intermediate-grade students.

# Read-Aloud Books

## Grades K–1

Brett, Jan. *The Mitten.*
Cannon, Janell. *Stellaluna.*
dePaola, Tomie. *Strega Nona.*
Duke, Kate. *Aunt Isabel Tells a Good One.*
Fleming, Denise. *In the Tall, Tall Grass.*
Freeman, Don. *Corduroy.*
Lester, Helen. *Hooway for Wodney Wat.*
Martin, Bill. *Brown Bear, Brown Bear, What Do You See?*
Mayer, Mercer. *There's a Nightmare in my Closet.*
Rosen, Michael. *We're Going on a Bear Hunt.*
Sendak, Maurice. *Where the Wild Things Are.*
Viorst, Judith. *Alexander and the Terrible, Horrible, No Good, Very Bad Day.*
Waber, Bernard. *Ira Sleeps Over.*
White, E. B. *Charlotte's Web.*
Wood, Audrey. *The Napping House.*

## Grades 2–3

Allard, Harry. *Miss Nelson Is Missing.*
Avi. *Finding Providence: The Story of Roger Williams.*
Cooney, Barbara. *Eleanor.*
Dahl, Roald. *James and the Giant Peach.*
Dicamillo, Kate. *The Tale of Despereaux.*
Fleischman, Sid. *The Whipping Boy.*
Ganeri, Anita. *Eruption! The Story of Volcanoes.*
Gibbons, Gail. *Spiders.*
Giff, Patricia Reilly. *The Beast in Mrs. Rooney's Room.*
Hoffman, Mary. *Amazing Grace.*
Robinson, Barbara. *The Best School Year Ever.*
Sachar, Louis. *Sideways Stories from Wayside School.*
Lovell, Patty. *Stand Tall, Molly Lou Melon.*
VanAllsburg, Chris. *Polar Express.*
Winthrop, Elizabeth. *The Castle in the Attic.*
Yolen, Jane. *Owl Moon.*

## Grades 4–6

Banks, Lynn Reid. *The Indian in the Cupboard.*
Black, Wallace B. and Blashfield, Jean F. *Pearl Harbor!*
Cleary, Beverly. *Dear Mr. Henshaw.*
Clements, Andrew. *Frindl.*
Creech, Sharon. *Love that Dog.*
Cooper, Susan. *Dark is Rising.*
Dicamillo, Kate. *Because of Winn Dixie.*
Gardiner, John. *Stone Fox.*

Parks, Rosa (with James Haskins). *Rosa Parks: My Story.*
Paterson, Katherine. *Bridge to Terabithia.*
Peck, Richard. *Fair Weather.*
Rathmann, Peggy. *Ruby the Copycat.*
Rawls, Wilson. *Where the Red Fern Grows.*
Sachar, Louis. *Holes.*
Scieszka, Jon and Smith, Lane. *Math Curse.*
Spinelli, Jerry. *Maniac Magee.*
Tsuchiya, Yukio. *Faithful Elephants.*
Twain, Mark. *Tom Sawyer.*

## Grades 7–8

Adler, David A. *The Babe and I.*
Bunting, Eve. *Terrible Thing: An Allegory of the Holocaust.*
Clements, Andrew. *The Landry News.*
Cushman, Karen. *Catherine Called Birdy.*
Davis, Kenneth. *Don't Know Much About American History.*
Hiaasen, Carl. *Hoot.*
Hinton, S. E. *The Outsiders.*
Konigsburg, E. L. *Silent to the Bone.*
Lester, Julius. *From Slave Ship to Freedom Road.*
Lowry, Lois. *The Giver.*
Paulsen, Gary. *Hatchet.*
Polacco, Patricia. *The Bee Tree.*
Snicket, Lemony. *The Series of Unfortunate Events.*
Woodson, Jacqueline. *Hush.*
Yolen, Jane. *Girl in a Cage.*

## Grades 9–12

Albom, Mitch. *Tuesdays with Morrie.*
Blanco, Jodee. *Please Stop Laughing at Me.*
Clements, Andrew. *Things Not Seen.*
Crutcher, Chris. *King of the Mild Frontier: An Ill-Advised Autobiography.*
Freedman, Russell. *The Life and Death of Crazy Horse.*
Hobbs, Will. *Downriver.*
Kidd, Sue Monk. *The Secret Life of Bees.*
Kingsolver, Barbara. *The Bean Trees.*
Konigsburg, E. L. *Silent to the Bone.*
Korman, Gordon. *Son of the Mob.*
Levitin, Sonia. *Cure.*
Oates, Joyce Carol. *Big Mouth, Ugly Girl.*
Paulsen, Gary. *Woodsong.*
Reisert, Rebecca. *Third Witch.*
Spinelli, Jerry. *Stargirl.*
Wolff, Virginia. *True Believer.*

# Language Experience

The Language Experience approach involves writing down what students say, then reading and rereading it with them to develop knowledge of letter-sound associations, sight words, prosody, and language (Mallon & Berglund, 1984; Stauffer, 1980; Strickland, Ganske, & Monroe, 2002). Stories created in this manner are usually placed in a prominent location in the classroom or bound into class books to be used as text material for independent reading. Students can generally read language experience stories successfully because they have participated in their development. Because the text reflects the language, culture, and experiences of the students, lessons using these materials are especially appropriate for English language learners (Herrell, 2000).

## PROCEDURE ▶◆◆

1. Gather students near an easel with chart paper or a chalkboard. Provide an experience or discuss something that is of current interest to students, such as a field trip, holiday, recent event, classroom pet, or picture.

2. As students describe the experience or topic, encourage them to use complete sentences. Repeat what is said and write it down, saying each word as you write it. Include the speaker's name as in the following example.

   Mark said, "The guinea pig was sleeping this morning."

3. After writing each sentence, read it aloud smoothly and expressively. Ask the speaker, "Is this what you meant to say? Did I write it the way you said it?" Make changes as needed. Invite students to read the sentence with you.

4. Invite students to dictate additional sentences. Reread them to and with students. Additional comments about the guinea pig might be as follows.

   Emily said, "I hope it is OK."

   Erica added, "I had a guinea pig once and it slept during the day, too."

   Jerry said, "I don't think we should worry. He is probably OK."

   Tyrone said, "Let's look at him again tomorrow and see if he is asleep again."

   "If he is, I think we will feel better," offered Shaunice.

5. When the story appears to be finished, read it to students, modeling good oral reading. Ask students to read along with you. Sweep your hand under the words as they are read.

6. Ask, "Is there anything else we should add? Have we written the story just the way we want it? Do you think someone who reads the story will understand our message?" This is an important time to emphasize that reading can be talk written down, and that the purpose of speaking and writing is to communicate a message.

7. On successive days, read the story chorally (see page 46) with students. Ask individual students to choose a sentence or sentences to read aloud. If a student has difficulty with a word, provide assistance. Celebrate when students read with appropriate speed, accuracy, and expression.

8. Post the story in a prominent place in the classroom or place it in a class book so that students can read and reread it independently. Invite students to add illustrations to enhance meaning and add interest for the reader.

# Phonemic Awareness

**DESCRIPTION**

In recent years phonological and phonemic awareness have been recognized as important factors in learning to read (National Reading Panel, 2000). Phonological awareness involves the ability to hear syllables, onsets, and rimes in spoken words. Phonemic awareness is one aspect of phonological awareness (Yopp & Yopp, 2000). Phonemic awareness refers to the ability to notice, think about, and work with the individual sounds (phonemes) in spoken words (Armbruster, Lehr, & Osborn, 2001). When students begin to associate these spoken sounds with the letters, they are linking their phonemic knowledge to their written form, the grapheme. This becomes phonics. Phonics is the understanding of how sounds relate to letters and how our written language system works (Armbruster, Lehr, & Osborn, 2001). To put it concisely, phonological awareness and phonemic awareness in themselves do not involve print, phonics does. Because of its common use in the literature and in professional discussions, the term phonemic awareness will be used.

## Why Phonemic Awareness Is Important

It has been suggested that phonemic awareness is a potent predictor of success in learning to read (Stanovich, 1986; Cunningham, 1990; Lundberg, Frost, & Peterson, 1988) and that its absence predicts the likelihood of failure in learning to read (Adams, 1990). Helping students become aware of the phoneme, the smallest unit of speech, leads to the development of an understanding of the alphabetic principle, an important prerequisite to being able to decode written words. Several studies have found that combining phonemic awareness activities with letter-sound instruction can be especially supportive of students' developing understanding of the alphabetic principle (Bradley & Bryant, 1983; Byrne & Fielding-Barnsley, 1993; Hohn & Ehri, 1983).

## Developmental Progression

The following progression of skills, suggested by Ehri, Nunes, Willows, Schuster, Yaghoub-Zadeh, and Shanahan (2001) and Blachman (2000), shows how students move from early to deep awareness of phonemes on their way to becoming skilled readers.

Students who are becoming phonemically aware increasingly demonstrate the ability to perform the eleven tasks described on the next page.

**Recognize that sentences are composed of individual words.**
(How many words are in this sentence? The dog went in his house. Clap each word.)

**Recognize and produce rhyming words.**
(Do these words rhyme? Can, fan, van. Can you say another word that rhymes with these words?)

**Recognize and produce syllables.**
(How many syllables to you hear in this word? Peanut. Clap each syllable. Can you say another two-syllable word? Clap each syllable.

**Recognize and produce onsets and rimes.**
(How are these words alike? Flake, flip, flat? Can you say another word that begins with /fl/? How are ride, hide, side alike? Can you think of another word that ends with /ide/?)

**Recognize and produce words with the same initial sound.**
(What sound to you hear at the beginning of these words? Paper, pen, pencil. Can you say another word that starts with the /p/ sound?)

**Recognize and produce words with the same ending sound.**
(What sound do you hear at the end of these words? Pen, can, fun. Can you say another word that ends with the /n/ sound?)

**Recognize oddity.**
(Which word is not like the others? Bag, nine, beach, bat.)

**Blend individual phonemes to make a word.**
(What word do we have when we put these sounds together c/a/t?)

**Segment words into their individual sounds.**
(What sounds do you hear in up?)

**Substitute or add phonemes to a word.**
(What word would we have if we added an /m/ to eat? What word would we have if we changed the /m/ to /b/? If we changed the /t/ to /m/? If we added an /s/ at the end?)

**Recognize and produce words with one phoneme deleted.**
(What word would we have if we left the /t/ off the end of seat?)

# Instructional Considerations

It is important to remember that phonemic awareness instruction is only one part of a rich literacy program. Students can develop sensitivity to the sound structure of language through the use of songs, chants, and word play activities. When phonemic awareness skills are specifically taught, it may be important to teach one skill at a time and demonstrate how the skill applies to reading or spelling (Ehri, et al., 2001). Instruction should generally consist of no more than twenty hours over the course of the school year, with individual sessions consisting of thirty minutes or less (Ehri, et al., 2001; Stanovich 1993).

# Basic Sight Vocabulary

◆◇◆ **DESCRIPTION** ◆◇◆◇◆◇◆◇◆◇◆◇◆◇◆◇◆◇◆◇◆◇◆◇◆◇◆

Reading fluency problems of students who struggle in reading occur primarily because of "their difficulties forming large vocabularies of words that they can recognize 'by sight' or at a single glance" (Torgesen & Hudson, 2006, p. 152). There are about 200 basic sight words that occur over and over in the English language (Johns, 1976). These words can comprise over 60% of the words used in beginning reading materials and over 50% of the words used in materials in the upper grades and beyond (including materials read by adults). This explains why the words are commonly referred to as *basic, high-frequency,* or *function* words. Students need to know these words automatically if they are to become fluent readers. Such words are a necessary, but not sufficient, condition for efficient reading. They are often difficult for students to learn because many of the words look similar, are abstract, and are not considered "regular" in pronunciation. Two basic word lists are provided for your use. The Revised Dolch List (1976) and High-Frequency Nouns (Johns, 1975) can be found on page 34 and page 35 respectively. They provide words for teaching and practice. Below are some tips for teaching and practicing basic sight words. Several additional strategies are offered by Elish-Piper, Johns, and Lenski (2006).

## Ideas for Instruction and Practice

1. **Create Instructional Materials.** Use words from the Revised Dolch List (Figure 2.2) and the High-Frequency Nouns (Figure 2.3) to create phrases, sentences, and short stories that students can read and reread to learn the words and gain confidence. You might want to invite older students to use the lists to prepare materials that can be used by their peers or younger students in a different grade. The phrases and sentences can be written on cards. The stories can be bound into simple little books and illustrated by the student who authored the book or the student who reads the book. Provide repeated opportunities for students to read the materials individually, with partners, and at home. Stress the need to read accurately with expression. Model as needed. Examples are shown below.

    *Phrases*
    by the road
    over by the school

    *Sentences*
    What time of the year is it?
    Her work was done very well.
    That thing has two heads!

*Short Story (A little book with a line on each page)*

My Father

I have a father.
He is a good man.
He works in a big city.
He gives me money.
Next year, he will get a new blue car.
It is time for me to go home from school.
My father will be at home.
He is going to get me a little dog.
The dog will be a good friend.
My father and I will play with him.
What should I call my dog?

2. **Use Pattern Books.** Select a particular pattern book that contains the word or words you want to help students learn or practice. There are many pattern books, and a large listing of such books can be found in Johns and Lenski (2005). Read the book aloud to students and, if possible, use a big book version so students can follow along. Reread the book, inviting students to read along, as they are able. You may wish to point to each word as it is read. Provide opportunities for students to take turns reading the book to each other. Later, you could prepare sentence strips with words from the pattern book and invite students to read the text from the sentence strips. The sentence strips could be cut up, and students could rearrange the words in order and read the sentence. Stress the need for meaningful phrasing and attention to punctuation. Older students could be invited to share some of the pattern books with younger students, thus helping to develop reader confidence.

3. **Teach Words Explicitly.** Students may persistently misread some of the basic sight words. Note the troublesome words and develop lessons to teach the words. Write the word on the chalkboard; students can write the word on a card. Chant the word. Then spell the word and say it as a class two or three times (e.g., w-e-n-t, went, w-e-n-t, went, w-e-n-t, went). Write several sentences on the chalkboard with a blank space for the word being learned. Invite students to read the sentence silently and then ask a volunteer to print the missing words in the sentence. Have the sentence read aloud, using good phrasing and expression. You should also model for students as needed. A few examples are shared below.

    Joann and Cheyenne _____ to the soccer game.

    I _____ to see my friend, Javon.

    I hit the ball and it _____ about ten feet!

    Do you know where she _____ ?

Students can also be invited to find the troublesome words in materials they read. Because basic sight words appear frequently, help students understand that knowing such words will enable them to read more quickly and easily.

# Revised Dolch List

| | | | | | |
|---|---|---|---|---|---|
| a | could | he | might | same | told |
| about | cut | heard | more | saw | too |
| across | did | help | most | say | took |
| after | didn't | her | much | see | |
| toward | | | | | |
| again | do | here | must | she | try |
| all | does | high | my | short | turn |
| always | done | him | near | should | two |
| am | don't | his | need | show | under |
| an | down | hold | never | six | up |
| and | draw | hot | next | small | upon |
| another | eat | how | new | so | us |
| any | enough | I | no | some | use |
| are | even | I'm | not | soon | very |
| around | every | if | now | start | walk |
| as | far | in | of | still | want |
| ask | fast | into | off | stop | warm |
| at | find | is | oh | take | was |
| away | first | it | old | tell | we |
| be | five | its | on | ten | well |
| because | for | just | once | than | went |
| been | found | keep | one | that | were |
| before | four | kind | only | the | what |
| began | from | know | open | their | when |
| best | full | last | or | them | where |
| better | gave | leave | other | then | which |
| big | get | left | our | there | while |
| black | give | let | out | these | white |
| blue | go | light | over | they | who |
| both | going | like | own | think | why |
| bring | gone | little | play | this | will |
| but | good | long | put | those | with |
| by | got | look | ran | thought | work |
| call | green | made | read | three | would |
| came | grow | make | red | through | yes |
| can | had | many | right | to | yet |
| close | hard | may | round | today | you |
| cold | has | me | run | together | your |

**Figure 2.2**

The rationale and research for this list are described in Johns, J. L. (1976). Updating the Dolch basic sight vocabulary. *Reading Horizons, 16,* 104–111.

 # High-Frequency Nouns

| | | |
|---|---|---|
| air | girl | nothing |
| back | group | people |
| book | hand | place |
| boy | head | road |
| car | home | room |
| children | house | school |
| city | man | side |
| day | men | table |
| dog | money | thing |
| door | morning | time |
| cye | mother | top |
| face | Mr. | town |
| father | Mrs. | tree |
| feet | name | water |
| friend | night | way |
| | | year |

**Figure 2.3**

The development of this list is described in Johns, J. L. (1975). Dolch list of common nouns—A comparison. *The Reading Teacher, 28,* 338–340.

From Jerry L. Johns and Roberta L. Berglund, *Fluency: Strategies & Assessments* (3rd ed.). Copyright © 2006 Kendall/Hunt Publishing Company (1-800-247-3458, ext. 4 or 5). May be reproduced for noncommercial educational purposes.

# Word Identification

When students do not know words at sight (automatically), they need strategies for identifying such words. Often, these strategies are referred to as decoding strategies. Some of the most common decoding strategies are phonics, word patterns or phonograms, structural analysis (inflected endings like *s, es, ing,* and *ly,* compound words, prefixes, suffixes) and context (the words near the unknown word). Numerous books have information and teaching strategies for decoding (Elish-Piper, Johns, & Lenski, 2006; Fox, 2000; Johns & Lenski, 2005). For effective strategy instruction, intentional (explicit) teaching is necessary. A consistent finding of research is that "word identification development is involved in improving comprehension" (Breznitz, 2006, p. 43). The following strategies should strengthen students' word identification strategies.

## Phonics Instruction and Practice

Phonics gives students a means to associate sounds with letters and letter combinations so they can pronounce a word not known at sight. The 26 letters in the English alphabet can represent over 40 sounds or phonemes. Some of the phonic elements commonly taught include initial consonants, final consonants, consonant digraphs, long vowel sounds, and short vowel sounds.

1. **Synthetic (Explicit) Phonics.** Directly teach students the name of the letter and the sound associated with it. Begin with initial letter sounds. Teach additional letters and sounds. Then help students learn to blend the sounds to say a word (*kkk-aaa-ttt* is *cat*). Provide numerous opportunities to practice the sounds taught. For example, use oral sentences and have students identify the word that begins with a particular sound (e.g., Help me identify some words at a birthday party that begin with *kkk*).

2. **Analytic (Deductive) Phonics.** Begin with some words students have in their oral vocabularies that start with the same letter sound (e.g., *bbb*—Bob, Bill, Beth, bee, bat, ball). As students offer words, write the words on the board under an uppercase or lowercase *b*. Use pictures and objects to stimulate students' backgrounds. Once the words are listed, help students understand the notion that *b* represents the same sound at the beginning of each word. Be explicit in making the connection between the letter and the sound. You might run your hand along each word as you say it, emphasizing the initial sound. Then invite students to add additional words to the list. Practice by saying some words that begin and do not begin with the sound taught. Students should listen and raise their hands when the word begins with the sound that is being taught.

3. **Alphabet Phonics.** Use alphabet books to help students learn and identify specific sounds. Read a selected page aloud and tell students which words begin with a specific sound. Do the same thing with the same letter in another alphabet book. Have students help you identify the words that begin with the same sound. Then have students suggest other words. To help practice, students can make their own alphabet books, a page at a time, as letters and sounds are taught. Magazine illustrations and drawn pictures can be used to help illustrate the page. Refer to Elish-Piper, Johns, and Lenski (2006) for additional ideas and a master alphabet page that can be reproduced and used to make alphabet books.

# Word Pattern (Phonograms) Instruction and Practice

Some words are made up of an onset and rime (*hill* = the onset *h* and the rime *-ill*). Another name for rimes is phonograms. Some of the rimes that can be taught for short vowel sounds are listed in the box below. Rimes for the long vowel sounds can be found in Johns and Lenski (2005).

| -ab | -ack | -ad, | -ag | -am | -amp | -an | -and | -ang | -ank | -ap | -ash | -atch | -eck | -ed | -eg | -ell |
|-----|------|------|-----|-----|------|-----|------|------|------|-----|------|-------|------|-----|-----|------|
| -ess | -est | -et | -ob | -ock | -od | -od | -ong | -op | -ot | -ib | -ick | -id | -ift | -ig | -ill | -im |
| -in | -ing | -ink | -ip | -ish | -it | -itch | -ub | -uck | -ud | -uff | -ug | -ull | -um | -ump | -un | -unch |
| -ung | -up | -ush | | | | | | | | | | | | | | |

1. **Nursery Rhymes and Poetry.** Select nursery rhymes or poetry that contain rhyming words (e.g., "Jack and Jill"). Tell students that some words rhyme (sound the same at the end). Then have students listen for rhyming words as you read "Jack and Jill." Invite sharing about the rhyme and ask students to identify words that rhyme. Write the words on the board under each other. Guide students as necessary. Then help students identify the rime (*-ill*) and help them see how they can use this word part to help identify other words with the same part (e.g., *bill, fill, pill, drill*). Provide additional practice by supplying additional initial sounds and having students add *-ill* to make new words (e.g., *will, mill, gill, still, spill, quill*). Once the words are identified, use pictures or simple words to help students understand any word meanings that may be unknown. Students can also be encouraged to relate the words to their lives.

2. **Phonogram Instruction.** Choose a word that contains an onset and rime (e.g., *hay*). Write a sentence on the board containing the word: *Cows eat hay.* Read the sentence and underline the *–ay* sound. Tell students that they can probably make other words that have an *–ay* sound. Model an example (If h-a-y spells *hay,* what do you think d-a-y spells?). Then write the new word on the board. Provide several additional examples, inviting students to tell you the new word (e.g., *jay, lay, pay, bay, ray, say, clay, play, tray, stay*). Then write sentences for each of the new words, clarifying meanings as needed. Introduce additional word patterns to help students learn more word patterns that can be used to help decode words.

3. **Making Words.** Many easy-to-use lessons in making words have been provided by Cunningham and Hall (1994a, 1994b, 1997a, 1997b, 1998). These lessons have students use letter tiles or letter cards to make words. Using the letters for a rime (e.g., *-ine*) and additional letters (d, f, l, m, n, p, v), tell students that you can use *-ine* and make words by adding a letter to the rime. Model an example and then have students make words independently using their individual letters. Once all the words have been written on the board, point out the similar features and stress that this knowledge can be used to help decode unknown words that have a similar pattern. You may want to extend the lesson by encouraging students to see how many different words they can make using two or more of the letters in any combination. Have students work individually or with partners and write their new words on a sheet of paper. Be sure to correct misspelled words and clarify word meanings as needed.

# Structural Analysis Instruction and Practice

*The Literacy Dictionary* (Harris & Hodges, 1995) defines structural analysis as "the identification of roots, affixes, compounds, hyphenated forms, inflected and derived endings, contractions, and in some cases, syllabication. Structural analysis is sometimes used as an aid to pronunciation or in combination with phonic analysis in word-analysis programs" (pp. 244–245). Obviously, there's a lot to structural analysis! We have chosen to provide some instructional assistance for inflected and derived endings (e.g., *s, es, ed, ly*), compound words, and roots with affixes (prefixes and suffixes). For further resources consult Elish-Piper, Johns, and Lenski (2006), Fox (2000), and Johns and Lenski (2005).

1. **Inflected and Derived Endings.** Inflected and derived endings are the *s, es, ed, ly, ing* and other endings that can be added to a word. Younger students may have difficulty recognizing known words like *want* that have an *s, ed,* or *ing* added. Older students may have trouble identifying longer words like *agreement* because of the *ment.* To help students identify words with inflected endings, begin with a word students know (e.g., fish, play, want, jump, laugh, record, help, end) and systematically model how you can identify word endings in an effort to identify the unknown word. Write *fishing* on the board and then think aloud to show students how you look for a known word with an ending. Identify the known word and then look at the ending. Underline the word and the ending. Pronounce each and then blend the two together to identify the word. Provide numerous examples to students, gradually increasing the difficulty. Then invite students to make new words adding inflected endings to words they already know (e.g., talk, talks, talked, talking).

2. **Compound Words.** Sometimes two smaller words are put together to make a longer word. Tell students that such words are called compound words. Write a sentence on the board that has a compound word (e.g., I got homesick when I went to camp.). Have students identify the longest word and tell them that it is a compound word. Then have students look for the smaller words to help them pronounce the longer word. Be explicit in helping students realize that when they are reading and they come across an unknown word, one strategy they can use is to look and see if it is made up of two smaller words. Provide additional compound words and see if students are able to identify them. Use the words in oral or written sentences and clarify word meaning as needed. The box below contains some compound words you may wish to use.

| | | | | | |
|---|---|---|---|---|---|
| afternoon | everyone | pancake | airplane | everything | peanut |
| wristwatch | overboard | notebook | dragonfly | downstairs | wildlife |
| firecracker | playground | quarterback | fireplace | backbone | anybody |
| highchair | grasshopper | neighborhood | oatmeal | uphill | checkerboard |
| horseshoe | jellybean | motorcycle | whirlpool | rollerblade | strawberry |
| basketball | dragonfly | fireworks | fingerprint | peppermint | turtleneck |

3. **Prefixes, Suffixes, and Root Words.** To help students decode polysyllabic words, teach them to look for prefixes and suffixes attached to base or root words. For example, *replacement* is made up of a prefix *(re),* base word *(place),* and suffix *(ment).* Sometimes students have little or no idea what to do in order to identify longer words like *replacement.* Write the word on the board and systematically show students the three parts. Identify each part using the appropriate terms. Tell students that when they come across a long word, they should look for a base or root word and a prefix and/or suffix. By separating the word into smaller parts, they can pronounce each part to try to say a word that they have heard before. Even if the word is not in their meaning vocabulary, they can use meanings for the

prefixes and suffixes to arrive at a possible meaning for the word. Model several examples by thinking aloud. Then provide some longer words in sentences and have students try to use prefixes, roots, and suffixes to pronounce the word. Build greater mastery by teaching common meanings for common prefixes and suffixes. You may want to begin with the four most common prefixes that help provide meanings to approximately 66% of the English words that have prefixes (Armbruster, Lehr, & Osborn, 2001). These four prefixes are *un-, re-, in-,* and *dis-*. Additional words you might want to use for instruction in longer words are found in the box below.

| | | | | | |
|---|---|---|---|---|---|
| replacement | nonliving | midnight | irresponsible | kindness | independence |
| hopeless | assistance | submarine | transportation | unfinished | valuable |
| composer | dishonest | expensive | inexpensive | indecent | indirect |
| ineligible | incorrect | inexact | unhappy | impractical | uncomfortable |
| illiterate | irreplaceable | uncovered | indivisible | inartistic | inequality |
| submarine | submerged | subnormal | subsonic | antifreeze | unsubscribe |
| unicycle | monocracy | monotone | biplane | biweekly | underlying |
| overflowed | undercooked | autograph | repay | retroactive | fearless |
| windowless | hopeless | spotless | blameless | endless | guiltless |
| sweetness | thickness | greatness | sickness | nearness | tenderness |

# Context Instruction and Practice

Context refers to "information from the immediate textual setting that helps identify a word or word group" (Harris & Hodges, 1995, p. 44). For example, you can probably add additional words to this phrase: Fourscore and seven years ago, _____. That's a powerful context. Students can also use context to anticipate or identify a word: "Bow wow," said the big brown _____ (dog). Context clues and minimal phonic clues can often be used in tandem to identify words: I saw birds in the s_____. The initial letter in the missing word makes it clear that the correct word cannot be *tree* and that it is probably *sky*. Helping students use context along with letter sounds can be an effective strategy for identifying words.

1. **Oral Context.** Before using the context in texts to help students identify unknown words, engage students in oral activities. Tell students that they can use what they already know to help identify words. Begin with several examples that are easy for your students (e.g., "Meow," said the _____ (cat, kitten, kitty). Encourage students to explain why they have chosen certain words. Provide additional oral examples where multiple answers will make sense (e.g., I like to eat _____). Write words students offer on the board and help students evaluate whether each word makes sense. Ask students to evaluate additional words you suggest, offering some words (e.g., cars, tires, bolts) that do not make sense. Be sure students understand that they can use their knowledge about words in their reading to say words that make sense.

2. **Written Context.** Print a sentence on the board with a missing word. Have students read the sentence and predict what the word is likely to be. Use an initial sentence that will be easy for your students: I heard a _____ bark last night. Have students identify clues in the sentence that helped them to identify the word. Then provide a sentence where multiple words are possible: The cat sat by the _____. Invite students to share words and justify them. Offer some additional words that do and do not make sense. Add a letter clue in the sentence where the blank is and have students narrow their choices to one or two words: The cat sat by the d_____ (door, dog). Help students refine their

predictions by offering additional letters until the word is known. Provide additional practice by offering clues for some words that are partially written on the board. Some possible examples are in the box below.

___ash (a name for money)
___ide (on the playground)
___pple (a fruit)

___eeth (you brush them)
___ike (you ride on it)
___oice (can be loud or soft)

___ent (name for a penny)
___en (write with it)
___ig (not small)

p___n (to fasten)
c___lf (baby cow)

ch___k (used for writing)
c___e (holds ice cream)

s___n (bright yellow)
f___ll (after summer)

hi___ (smaller than mountain)
di___ (worth ten cents)

cu___ (baby bear)
bo___ (you read it)

li___ (not dark)
ba___ (very small child)

3. **Context and Phonics.** Help students transfer the above strategies to their reading by using examples from enlarged texts and various reading selections in your curriculum. Select examples where a word in the text may be covered and easily identified because of the rich context. Then show the word to help students realize the power that context can have. Provide other examples where the context will permit more than one word to be suggested. Then gradually supply selected letters of the covered word to help students narrow their choices. Always encourage students to give reasons for their thinking before revealing the word. Sometimes students may be able to use the last line on a page and be able to predict the first word on the following page before turning the page. Help them realize that they are using context. Here's an actual example of a last line on a page from a book that one of us was reading: For each permissible combination of a word and suffix, write _____. Perhaps you also correctly predicted that *the* appeared at the top of the next page. You might also use examples from your own reading to help students realize the power of context and phonics identifying words.

# Shared Reading

# Shared Book Experience

## ◈◈◈ MATERIALS ►◆◆

◆ Enlarged text

◆ Small version of the enlarged text (optional)

## ◈◈◈ USE ►◆◆

◆ Whole Group

◆ Small Group

## ◈◈◈ DESCRIPTION ►◆◆◆ ◆◆◆◆◆◆◆◆◆◆◆◆◆◆◆◆◆◆◆◆◆◆◆◆◆◆◆

Sometimes viewed as a school version of the bedtime story, Shared Book Experience involves a teacher and a group of students sharing reading by listening to and rereading stories, rhymes, songs, and poems in an enjoyable manner (Berglund, 1988; Butler & Turbill, 1985; Holdaway, 1979). Shared Book Experience invites students into the reading process through the repeated sharing of materials that soon become favorites. Many insights about literacy can be taught from Shared Book Experiences. In order to increase visual intimacy with print, materials used for Shared Book Experiences are often enlarged books (big books) or text shared on the overhead projector. Books and stories with repetitive language patterns or predictable story structures are especially useful for this experience.

## ◈◈◈ PROCEDURE ►◆◆

1. **Reread old favorites.** Begin with familiar rhymes, songs, poems, or chants that students know. These can be chosen either by you or by your students. Because these favorites are familiar to students, they can actively participate in the reading, particularly when there is repetitive text. For instance, for very young children, the chant, "Brown Bear, Brown Bear, What do you see?" is easily learned and repeated as the teacher reads and rereads this book (Martin, 1987). Point to the text as you read so that students can see the print, learn print conventions (left-right, top-bottom, front-back, punctuation, spaces, title), and note the connection between written and spoken language.

2. **Introduce a new story.** At least once a week, introduce a new story. Show the cover of the book and invite students to predict what the story may be about. Share the title, author, and illustrator with students and note if other books by the same author or illustrator were shared in previous readings.

3. **Read the story aloud.** Read the story all the way through, modeling good rate and expression. You may wish to stop at exciting points and allow students to check predictions and make new ones. The purpose of this segment of the lesson is to allow students to enjoy the story.

4. **Discuss the story.** Return to the predictions made as a class and invite students to confirm or revise them. Discuss the illustrations, characters, and favorite or exciting parts of the story to help students understand the meaning of the text. This is also a good time for students to be invited to make connections between the new story and any previous texts (text-to-text) or connections between the story and their own experiences (text-to-self) (Keene & Zimmermann, 1997).

5. **Reread the story aloud.** Invite students to join in the reading. Students may read a repetitive segment with you and add appropriate sound effects or hand gestures to enhance meaning.

6. **Make the text available for independent reading.** Put the enlarged text and/or smaller versions of the text in a reading corner or literacy center and encourage students to read it independently or with a friend.

7. **Use the text again for familiar rereadings and for teaching reading strategies.** During another Shared Book Experience, draw from the story previously read and discussed; after reading it, use the text to teach and practice the following:
    - ✧ reading with expression and fluency
    - ✧ sight vocabulary
    - ✧ sound/symbol relationships
    - ✧ word families
    - ✧ effective reading strategies

8. **Encourage students to use the meaning of the story, how the language sounds, and letter-sound relationships to predict and self-correct their reading.** Use questions such as, "Does it make sense? Does it sound right? Does it look right?" to help students develop good fix-up strategies to use when the reading process breaks down.

Fluency practice might include inviting students to Echo Read the text with you (see page 44), discussing the use of typographic signals (Super Signals on page 50), practicing Phrase Boundaries (see page 52), or using Say It Like the Character (see page 90). Following the rereading of the text, it could be used again during Sustained Silent Reading (SSR) (see page 105) or Read and Relax (see page 102). For additional ideas for using big books and Shared Book Experience, see Strickland (1993).

### ✧✧✧ EVALUATION (student behaviors to look for) ▶✧✧
- ✧ Quality of predictions
- ✧ Text-to-text and text-to-self connections
- ✧ Accuracy of word identification
- ✧ Appropriate emphasis and expression

# Echo Reading

**MATERIALS**

✧ Reading selection

**USE**

✧ Whole Group
✧ Small Group

**DESCRIPTION**

Echo Reading involves modeling fluent reading for students and then encouraging them to reread, or echo, the same text, with support as needed. In Echo Reading, the student immediately echoes or imitates the performance of a more skilled reader. Doing so helps the student gain confidence in reading aloud, become proficient with material that might be too difficult for the student to read independently, and practice good phrasing and expression (Allington, 2001; Gillet, Temple, & Crawford, 2004).

**PROCEDURE**

1. For students' initial experiences with echo reading, select fairly easy reading material. Stories with patterns or repeated phrases and poetry are excellent for beginning the activity. Students' language experience stories (see page 28) are also good sources for echo reading materials.

2. Read a phrase or sentence of the selection aloud. Call attention to any textual signals that help you determine the rate and expression you used. For the sentence, " 'You're back!' Mama cried as her son walked through the door," you might say that the exclamation mark helped you know that you should read the sentence in an excited voice.

3. Reread the phrase or sentence and have students echo the same text immediately after you finish.

4. If students echo your reading effectively, mirroring your rate, accuracy, and expression, continue by modeling the next phrase or sentence. Then have students again echo your reading.

5. If students do not echo your reading effectively on the first try, model the phrase or sentence again and have students echo your reading again.

6. As students become proficient with easy materials, gradually move into more difficult materials.

## ◈◈◈ EVALUATION *(student behaviors to look for)* ▸◆◆

✧ Accuracy of word identification

✧ Appropriate rate

✧ Expression similar to that modeled

FLUENCY
GOALS
COMPREHENSION
ACCURACY
EXPRESSION
SPEED

# Choral Reading

 **MATERIALS**

✧ Reading selection

 **USE**

✧ Whole Group
✧ Small Group

**DESCRIPTION**

Choral Reading involves students reading a text in unison (Gillet, Temple, & Crawford, 2004). It helps build confidence and extend enjoyment of the reading process (Opitz & Rasinski, 1998). Repeated practice of choral reading materials helps to develop reading competence, nurtures collaboration among students, and helps students feel successful as readers.

**PROCEDURE**

1. Select a text for use in the Choral Reading experience. Poetry or books with predictable story patterns, repeated phrases, or refrains work especially well. See the suggested resources that follow.

2. Provide copies of the text to each student in the group, make a transparency of the text, and show it on the overhead projector or write the text on chart paper so that all can view it.

3. Read the text aloud to students, modeling fluent reading. Tell students why you chose to read it as you did. For example, were there punctuation marks that gave you clues? Perhaps there was bold print or underlining which gave you a clue about emphasis.

4. After your modeling, invite students to follow along and read with you. Practice reading together chorally several times.

5. You may wish to vary the Choral Reading experience by having students join in chorally for repeated refrains in the text. For instance, in the poem "The Jumblies" by Edward Lear in *Sing a Song of Popcorn* by deRegniers (1988), the refrain is one that students enjoy reading chorally, although the rest of the poem may be too difficult for them to read with fluency:

> Far and few, far and few,
> Are the lands where the Jumblies live;
> Their heads are green, and their hands are blue,
> And they went to sea in a Sieve.

6. A further adaptation of Choral Reading is Antiphonal Reading (see page 48) where students are divided into groups, with each group reading its assigned part.

## EVALUATION (student behaviors to look for)

✦ Accuracy of word identification

✦ Appropriate rate

✦ Expression similar to that modeled

## SUGGESTED RESOURCES
### for Choral Reading

Barton, B., & Booth, D. (1995). *Mother Goose goes to school.* Portland, ME: Stenhouse.
deRegniers, B. (1988). *Sing a song of popcorn: Every child's book of poems.* New York: Scholastic.
Prelutsky, J. (1984). *The new kid on the block.* New York: Greenwillow.
Prelutsky, J. (2000). *The random house book of poetry for children.* New York: Random House.
Silverstein, S. (1974). *Where the sidewalk ends.* New York: HarperCollins.

# Antiphonal Reading

**MATERIALS**

✧ Reading selection

**USE**

✧ Whole Group
✧ Small Group
✧ Partner

**DESCRIPTION**

Antiphonal Reading is an adaptation of choral reading. In Antiphonal Reading, students are usually divided into groups (Miccinati, 1985; Worthy & Broaddus, 2001/2002). Each group reads an assigned part—sometimes alternately, sometimes in unison. The manner of reading is cued by the placement of the text on the page. Usually Antiphonal Reading is done with poetry obtained from published sources or from materials students have created. Miccinati (1985) suggests that rhymes, limericks, sea chanties, and Indian chants are especially well suited to this activity.

**PROCEDURE**

1. Select the text to be read and make it visually accessible by providing copies for each student or showing it on the overhead projector. Some resources are listed on the following page.

2. Explain to students the unique way this material is written, for instance, in two columns, indicating how it should be read.

3. Model for students how Antiphonal Reading in two parts is done by inviting an able student who is a risk-taker to be your partner. You begin by reading the first segment of print on the left side of the page. Your partner then reads the first segment of his or her part on the right side of the page. If both sides of the page contain the same print on the same line, read that part in unison with your partner. Proceed through the entire selection, modeling good reading and the turn-taking that is involved in Antiphonal Reading. Point to the text as each of you read your respective parts so that the listeners understand the cues.

4. Now divide the students into two groups, with each group assigned either the left side or right side of the text.

5. Invite the groups to try reading the poem in the manner in which you and your partner have modeled it. Repeat the process several times, until students become proficient at reading their respective parts with fluency.

6. As a follow-up activity, you may wish to invite students to write poetry which follows the form introduced in Antiphonal Reading. On the following page is an example of a poem written in two parts by fourth-grade students.

### The Titanic

| | |
|---|---|
| Titanic | Titanic |
| | Hit an iceberg |
| Titanic | Titanic |
| Sank to the bottom of the sea | |
| Titanic | Titanic |
| Titanic | Titanic |
| Titanic | Titanic |
| | 1,025 people died |
| 700 people lived | |
| Titanic | Titanic |
| People went under water | |
| | To study the |
| Titanic | Titanic |
| | We want to know why |
| The Titanic sank | |
| Titanic | Titanic |
| Titanic | Titanic |
| Titanic | Titanic |
| | by Rebecca and Mike |

## ◈◈◈ EVALUATION (student behaviors to look for) ▸◆◈◆

✧ Accuracy of word identification

✧ Appropriate rate

✧ Expression similar to that modeled

## ◈◈◈ SUGGESTED RESOURCES ▸◆◈◆
### for Antiphonal Reading

Fleischman, P. (2000). *Big talk: Poems for four voices*. Cambridge, MA: Candlewick.

Fleischman, P. (1988). *Joyful noise: Poems for two voices*. New York: HarperCollins.

Fleischman, P. (1985). *I am Phoenix: Poems for two voices*. New York: HarperCollins.

Hoberman, M. A. (2001). *You read to me, I'll read to you: Very short stories to read together*. Boston: Little, Brown.

# Super Signals

### ⬥ MATERIALS ⬥⬥

✧ Various text selections

✧ Super Signals Chart (optional)

### ⬥ USE ⬥⬥

✧ Whole Group

✧ Small Group

### ⬥ DESCRIPTION ⬥⬥⬥

Super Signals involves helping students look for and understand the typographic signals that are used to help convey the author's message. Signals such as bold or italic type, commas, exclamation marks, and type size are often clues to meaning that should be noted by the reader, particularly during oral reading.

### ⬥ PROCEDURE ⬥⬥

1. Select a text that contains signals you wish to help students understand, for example, bold or enlarged type, exclamation marks, or italicized type.

2. Use a big book or enlarge the passage for use on an overhead projector.

3. Read the selection aloud to the students, allowing them to see the text as you read. During the first reading, use no expression, pauses, or changes in pitch.

4. Reread the same passage aloud, using differing pitches, pauses, and expression as indicated by the text.

5. Discuss with students the differences in the two readings. Encourage them to explain why you changed your reading the second time. Ask them which reading helped them better understand the text.

6. Encourage students to note the signals in the text that helped you know when to pause, raise your voice, or stop. Note how using these signals enhances understanding of the text.

7. Provide students with text that contains some of the Super Signals you have just modeled. Ask them to first read the text silently and then to read it aloud, showing that they understand the signals.

8. Tell students to look for Super Signals in their reading and use these important clues to gain the author's meaning.

9. You may wish to create a classroom chart of Super Signals. Invite students to share Super Signals that they locate in their reading materials and note how these signals are used to convey meaning (Opitz & Rasinski, 1998). A sample chart is shown below.

## Our Super Signals Chart

| SUPER SIGNAL | WHAT IT MEANS | EXAMPLE |
|---|---|---|
| Exclamation Mark ! | Excitement | "Think! Think!" |
| *Italics* | Emphasis | "But I want *more!* And I want *you* to make it for me!"<br>"Where did you get *this?*" he asked, showing her the gold. |
| Dash — | Pause | "You don't need them anymore—your people love you now." |
| Comma , | Pause<br>Cluster words between commas together as you read them. | And whenever the king started worrying about gold, she sent him on a goodwill trip throughout the countryside, which cheered him up. |

## EVALUATION (student behaviors to look for) ▶◆◆

◆ Increased awareness of typographic signals

◆ Appropriate use of typographic signals in text while reading

# Phrase Boundaries

 **MATERIALS**

✦ Reading selection

**USE**

✦ Whole Group

**DESCRIPTION**

One aspect of fluency involves clustering reading into appropriate phrases, rather than reading word by word. Appropriate phrasing helps the reader to understand the passage (Shanahan, 2000b). Cromer (1970) and O'Shea and Sindelar (1983) found that using text segmented into phrasal units resulted in improved comprehension, particularly for students who may be slow, but accurate, readers. Teaching students to read in phrases involves modeling appropriate phrasing, giving students guided practice in phrasing, and then moving toward independent practice in proper phrasing. Finally, students are invited to work with new materials to decide where phrase boundaries should be placed in order to enhance comprehension of the text. Rasinski (1990) found that the practice of marking phrase boundaries can lead to improved oral reading performance and comprehension, particularly for less-able students.

**PROCEDURE**

1. Provide copies of a phrase-cued text that has boundaries marked with a slash mark (/), or show the marked text on the overhead projector. You might wish to use one slash mark for phrases within a sentence and double slash marks at the end of a sentence. For example, "The ducks/ marched out of the park/ in a straight line."// or "Waving his arms frantically,/ he shouted at the driver to stop."//

2. Read the text aloud to students, demonstrating how you group the words together in each of the phrases.

3. Invite students to read the text aloud with you, grouping the words just as you have modeled.

4. After students appear to be successfully reading the text in phrases with you, have them read the text aloud individually or in pairs, remembering to continue to read in phrases.

5. On another day, give students copies of the material that has been practiced. Ask them to add slash marks to indicate the phrase boundaries. Have students check their phrasing by reading aloud to each other or to you. Their phrasing should be meaningful and should demonstrate comprehension of the passage.

6. When students appear to become more proficient at reading in phrases, provide copies of new materials to students. Ask them to read the materials and mark the phrase boundaries independently. To check the accuracy of their markings, have one or two students read aloud, using the phrases they have created. Allow students in the class to decide if the phrasing enhances comprehension. Shanahan (2000b) suggests that independent marking of such boundaries can be given as a homework assignment to older students.

## EVALUATION (student behaviors to look for)

✧ Ability to determine meaningful phrase boundaries

✧ Ability to cluster words into meaningful phrases when reading aloud

# Fluency Development Lesson

## MATERIALS

◇ Reading selection

## USE

◇ Whole Group
◇ Partner

## DESCRIPTION

The Fluency Development Lesson combines several oral reading strategies to create multiple opportunities for readers who struggle to hear and practice fluent reading (Rasinski & Padak, 1996). The lesson is designed to be used at least four times per week over an extended period of time, to encourage accurate word recognition and expression which ultimately contribute to thoughtful reading. This procedure involves reading to, with, and by students.

## PROCEDURE

1. Give students copies of a reading passage consisting of 50 to 200 words.

2. Read the text aloud while students follow along silently. This step may be repeated several times.

3. Discuss the content of the text with the students and encourage them to think about the way in which you read it aloud to them. Ask them how you used your voice, rate, and expression to help convey the meaning of the text.

4. Next, using Echo Reading (see page 44) and then Choral Reading (see page 46), have students read the text with you. It is important to continue to model fluent reading as students read with you and echo your reading.

5. When students appear to be developing proficiency and confidence in reading the text with you, have students form pairs.

6. Have student pairs move to various locations in the classroom. One student now reads the text aloud three times to his or her partner, while the partner follows along in the text. The listener provides help, if needed, and gives positive feedback such as, "You read all the words correctly," or "You really sounded excited when you read the part where they were running away from the bear."

7. Have students reverse roles so the reader becomes the listener and the listener becomes the reader. Repeat the above step.

8. Ask students to come back together as a whole group and ask for volunteers to read the text aloud to the entire group. At this time, the listeners do not follow along, but instead, enjoy the performance of their peers.

9. Praise students for their oral reading proficiency and their excellent listening behaviors.

10. Encourage students to take one copy of the passage home and read it to parents and relatives.

11. Put one copy of the passage into a notebook or folder for each student. Selected passages can be used for choral reading on successive days.

## EVALUATION (student behaviors to look for)

✧ Accuracy of word identification and self-correction behaviors

✧ Appropriate rate

✧ Appropriate expression

# Assisted Reading

# Paired Reading

 **MATERIALS** ◆◆

◆ Reading selection
◆ How Well Did Your Partner Read reproducible for each student (page 62 or 63)

 **USE** ◆◆

◆ Partner

**DESCRIPTION** ◆◆◆ ◆◆◆◆◆◆◆◆◆◆◆◆◆◆◆◆◆◆◆◆◆◆◆◆◆

Paired Reading, originally developed for use by parents and their children, is also a useful technique in the classroom (Topping, 1987a, 1987b, 1989). The tutor, a more capable reader, supports the tutee in reading materials that are generally more difficult than those read independently. In addition to supplying support in word recognition, the tutor also plays a major role in extending understanding of the text through discussion and questioning. Paired Reading has been found effective in improving accuracy and comprehension for students of all abilities between the ages of 6 and 13 (Topping, 1987a). The procedure for Paired Reading is easy to learn and implement in the classroom. Topping (1989) recommends that pairs work together three times per week for a minimum of six weeks, in sessions ranging from 15 to 30 minutes.

**PROCEDURE** ◆◆

1. Allow the tutee to select reading material within his or her instructional level.
2. Choose a comfortable place to read where both you and tutee can see the text easily (see Tips When Reading with Your Partner on page 60).
3. Begin by reading the text chorally (see page 46) at a speed that is comfortable for the tutee. If the tutee makes an error, say the word correctly. Have the tutee repeat the word and then proceed with choral reading. For example, if the tutee says "second" for "secret" in the sentence, "Gary promised to keep everything a secret," the tutor would stop reading and say "secret," the tutee would repeat the word "secret" and the pair would continue reading chorally.

4. If the tutee self-corrects a miscue, offer praise. Also praise the tutee if other self-monitoring behaviors are exhibited and for using good rate and prosody (stress, pitch, and phrasing).

5. If the text selected is at the tutee's independent reading level, the tutee can choose to read it aloud without the support of the tutor. When the tutee uses a prearranged signal (e.g., a tap or nudge) stop reading chorally with the tutee.

6. If the tutee encounters a difficult word, wait for five seconds. If the tutee does not correctly read the word, provide the word and return to reading chorally with the tutee.

7. Continue reading chorally until the tutee again signals that he or she wishes to read without support.

8. At the completion of the session, talk with the tutee about reading behaviors that are improving (see Here are Some Things You Might Say to Your Partner on page 60). Note progress on the Paired Reading Record Sheet (see page 61) and/or on the sheets titled How Well Did Your Partner Read? (see pages 62–63).

## EVALUATION (student behaviors to look for)

✧ Quality of discussion about the selection

✧ Accuracy of word identification and self-correction behaviors

✧ Improvement in the items listed on the How Well Did Your Partner Read reproducible

# Tips When Reading with Your Partner

1. Sit closely enough together so that you can speak quietly to each other.
2. Sit so that you can both see the print.
3. Follow along when your partner is reading.
4. Encourage your partner.

# Here Are Some Things You Might Say to Your Partner

1. You read that smoothly.
2. You read at a speed that sounded just right.
3. You read the words correctly.
4. You noticed the punctuation.
5. You remembered what you read.
6. You read with expression.
7. You are really improving!

 **Paired Reading Record**

Tutor _____ Tutee _____

| DATE | MATERIAL READ | BEHAVIORS NOTED | MINUTES OF READING (CIRCLE ONE) |
|------|---------------|-----------------|--------------------------------|
|      |               |                 | 5  10  15<br>20  25  30 |
|      |               |                 | 5  10  15<br>20  25  30 |
|      |               |                 | 5  10  15<br>20  25  30 |
|      |               |                 | 5  10  15<br>20  25  30 |
|      |               |                 | 5  10  15<br>20  25  30 |

# How Well Did Your Partner Read?

| | | | | Comments & Suggestions for Improvement |
|---|---|---|---|---|
| 1. | Did your partner read more smoothly? | Yes | No | _____ |
| | | | | _____ |
| 2. | Did your partner read more quickly? | Yes | No | _____ |
| | | | | _____ |
| 3. | Did your partner read more words correctly? | Yes | No | _____ |
| | | | | _____ |
| 4. | Did your partner use the punctuation better? | Yes | No | _____ |
| | | | | _____ |
| 5. | Did it sound like it made sense? | Yes | No | _____ |
| | | | | _____ |
| 6. | Did your partner read with more expression? | Yes | No | _____ |

What was the biggest area of need for your partner? _____

_____

What was the biggest improvement that your partner made? _____

_____


_____  _____  _____
    Your name/signature            Partner's name/signature            Date

# How Well Did Your Partner Read?

Tutor _____ Tutee _____

What We Read _____ Date _____

Check (✓) what your partner did while reading.

_____ Read Smoothly      _____ Read Quickly

_____ Knew Most Words      _____ Used Punctuation Correctly

_____ Used Good Expression      _____ Sounded Like Talking

Tell your partner one thing that was better about his or her reading.




Have your partner circle the word or words that tells how well he or she thinks the reading went.

Terrible      Not So Good      OK      Good      Great

Choose one thing to work on next time you read together and write it below.

_____

Comments:

_____

_____

# Neurological Impress Method

**MATERIALS**

✦ Reading selection

**USE**

✦ Partner

**DESCRIPTION**

The Neurological Impress Method involves the teacher and the student reading aloud simultaneously from the same book (Heckelman, 1969). The teacher reads slightly faster than the student to keep the reading fluent. The teacher usually sits next to the student and focuses his or her voice near the ear of the student. The goal is to help the student engage in a fluent reading experience. This method offers some of the guidance mentioned by the National Reading Panel (2000).

**PROCEDURE**

1.  Select an interesting book or passage that is appropriate for the student's reading level. It is recommended that you begin with easy reading materials that the student can read with at least 95% accuracy. You might want the student to choose materials from among several appropriate pre-selected items.

2.  Relate the need to practice reading to some activity in which the student participates (e.g., soccer, swimming, or art). Stress that practice is necessary to excel in many activities, such as sports and reading. Tell the student that you will help the student practice by reading with him or her.

3.  Have the student sit slightly in front of you so that your voice is close to the student's ear. Begin by reading the selected material out loud together. You should read a *little* louder and faster than the student.

4.  Run your finger under the words simultaneously as the words are read. Have the student assume this task when he or she is confident enough. Make sure that print, finger, and voice operate together. You may want to assist the student by placing your hand over the student's and guiding it smoothly.

5. Reread the initial lines or paragraph several times together to build confidence and comfort with the method before proceeding to new material. As the passage is reread, drop your voice behind the student's, if you think he or she is gaining fluency.

6. Read for two to three minutes in the initial sessions. The goal should be to establish a fluent reading pattern. Appropriate intonation and expression in reading are vital. The major concern is with the style of the reading.

7. Supplement the Neurological Impress Method with Echo Reading (see page 44) if the student has extreme difficulty with saying a word or phrase. Say the phrase and have the student repeat the phrase. When the student has satisfactorily repeated the phrase several times, return to the book or passage.

8. From time to time, speed up the pace for just a few minutes. Heckelman (1969) suggests using the Neurological Impress Method daily for up to fifteen minutes to provide a total of ten hours of assistance. An alternative might be to use the method several times a week for several months. A paraprofessional or volunteer might be trained to work with individual students—especially those who struggle in reading.

## EVALUATION (student behaviors to look for)

✧ Quality of phrasing and expression

✧ Increase in confidence while reading

# Preview-Pause-Prompt-Praise

**MATERIALS**

✧ Reading selection

**USE**

✧ Partner

**DESCRIPTION**

Preview-Pause-Prompt-Praise is a peer tutoring technique used to develop self-monitoring and fluent reading (Allington, 2001; Corso, Funk, & Gaffney, 2001/2002; Topping, 1987b). Pairs of students, often of differing ages or reading abilities, read together from the same text and support each other through the reading by using the Preview-Pause-Prompt-Praise technique. Allington (2001) recommends that parents, teachers, teaching assistants, and peers use a similar strategy when listening to students read aloud.

**PROCEDURE**

1. Pair students with older or more able reading tutors.

2. The tutor *previews* the reading, by discussing the cover and title of the book with the reader and then posing the question, "What do you think this will be about?" Several brief ideas may be shared with reasons offered. (See Tutor Guide on page 68.)

3. The tutee then begins reading aloud while the tutor listens, or the pair may read the first few sentences together chorally. If the reading is done chorally, the tutor discontinues reading along after the first few sentences, and the tutee continues to read aloud to the tutor.

4. If the tutee miscalls a word or appears to be having difficulty, the tutor should *pause* for three to five seconds to wait for the student to self-correct or read to the end of the sentence.

5. If the reader does not make a self-correction, decode the word, or reread the sentence correctly, the tutor provides *prompts* to assist the reader. For example:

   ✧ If the word does not make sense, the tutor prompts with a clue to the meaning by saying, "Does that make sense? Does it sound right? What word would sound right?"

   ✧ If the word makes sense, but it is incorrect, the tutor might prompt the tutee to look more carefully at the letters in the word by saying, "What does the word start with? Do you see a part of the word that you know? Can you reread, say the first sound, and see if the word falls out of your mouth?"

   ✧ If the tutee stops, the tutor might say, "Go back to the beginning of the sentence and try reading it again."

   ✧ If, after two prompts, the tutee still does not correct the problem, the tutor tells the tutee the word.

6. If the tutee self-corrects, or in some way fixes the problem, the tutor *praises* the tutee and invites him or her to continue reading.

7. After reading, the tutor *praises* something the tutee did well. For example, "I noticed that you stopped and went back when what you were reading didn't seem to make sense. That's something that good readers do."

8. The reading time concludes with the tutor asking, "What was your favorite part?" The tutor may also wish to share his or her favorite part as well.

## ✧✧✧ EVALUATION (student behaviors to look for) ▸✦✦

✧ Quality of predictions

✧ Accuracy of word identification and self-correction behaviors

✧ Quality of sharing after reading

# Tutor Guide

Tutor _____ Name of Reader _____

Title of Selection _____ Date _____

1. **To Begin**

   **Preview:** Look at the cover and title of the book. Ask, **"What do you think this will be about?"**

   **"Let's start by reading together. When I stop reading along with you, you should keep reading."**

2. **During Reading**

   **Prompt:** If the reader struggles and does not fix a problem, **Pause and slowly count to five.** Then you might **Prompt** by saying the following:

   **Does that make sense?**

   **Does that look right?**

   **Does that sound right?**

3. **After Reading**

   **Praise:** Tell the reader about something he or she did well. You might say, **"I noticed how you went back and figured out the word that you struggled with."**

   Ask, **"What was your favorite part?"**

   Then offer your favorite part. You might say, **"I really liked this part the best."** If your favorite part is the same one the reader chose, you might say, **"I liked that part, too!"**

# Structured Repeated Reading

## MATERIALS

✧ Reading selection

✧ Reading Progress Chart reproducible for each student (page 72)

✧ Stopwatch or watch with a second hand

✧ Calculator (recommended)

## USE

✧ Individual

## DESCRIPTION

The method of Structured Repeated Reading is a motivational strategy that engages students in repeated readings of text (Samuels, 1979). A Reading Progress Chart helps monitor the student's growth in fluency, which results, in part, from the automatic recognition of words and the reduction of miscues. Engaging students in repeated readings of text "is particularly effective in fostering more fluent reading" for students "struggling to develop proficient reading strategies" (Allington, 2001, p. 73). This specific instructional approach was among those mentioned by the National Reading Panel (2000) as an effective practice. The following procedure has been adapted from Johns and Lenski (2005).

## PROCEDURE

1. Select a brief passage or story of 50 to 200 words for the student to read aloud. For beginning readers or readers who struggle, a passage of approximately 50 words is sufficient for the first time the strategy is used. The passage should be at an appropriate level of difficulty. That means that the student should generally recognize more than 90% of the words. If the passage contains 50 words, the student should generally recognize about 45 of the words. If the student misses more than 6 words in a 50-word passage, it is probably not suitable for use in repeated reading experiences.

2. Ask the student to read the passage orally. Using a copy of the passage, note the student's miscues and keep track of the time (in seconds) it took the student to read the passage.

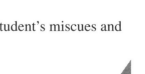

3.  Ask the student to tell you something about the passage or ask a question or two. Be sure that the student is not just calling words.

4.  Record the time in seconds and the number of miscues as in the sample below. In the example in the sidebar, the student read a 45-word passage in 58 seconds and made 4 miscues. To convert seconds into rate in words per minute (WPM), multiply the number of words in the passage by 60 and then divide by the time (in seconds) it took the student to read the passage. As noted in the example, the rate is approximately 46 words per minute (WPM).

$$\begin{array}{r} 46\ \text{WPM} \\ 58\overline{)2700} \\ 232 \\ \hline 380 \\ 348 \\ \hline \end{array}$$

5.  Encourage the student to practice rereading the passage independently for a day or two. The reading can be done both orally and silently. It can also be done at home. The goal is to have the student practice the passage several times before you next meet with the student to repeat the process described in Step 2.

6.  Repeat the process of having the student read the passage to you. Record the time in seconds and the number of miscues on the chart under Reading 2. Continue this general procedure over a period of time, until a suitable rate is achieved. You can use your professional judgment to determine a suitable rate or refer to the norms or targets for oral-reading rates provided on pages 6 and 8. The chart on the next page shows the five readings for a second-grade student over a 10-day period. The initial rate of 46 WPM was increased to approximately 87 WPM by the fifth reading. According to the norms provided for second graders in the spring of the year (see page 6), this student's rate is slightly below average.

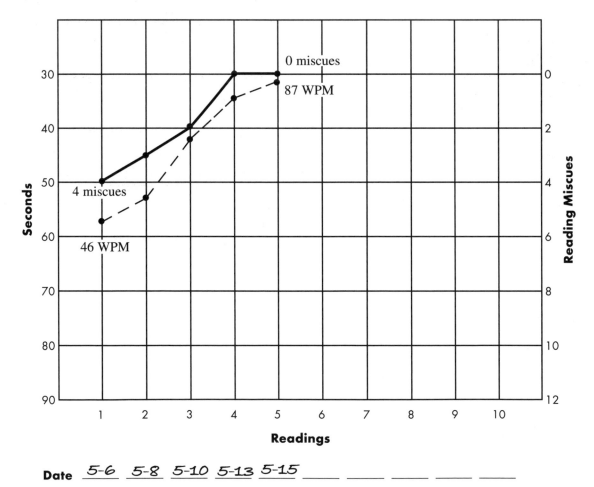

7. Repeat the strategy with a new selection. As you use the Reading Progress Chart on page 72, note that space is provided to record the date and to chart up to ten readings. You should base the actual number of readings on the student's progress in fluency. Some students will achieve a satisfactory level of fluency after a few readings; other students may need six or seven readings. Be flexible and responsive to individual differences. The Reading Progress Chart was designed to show visible evidence of gains. Students are encouraged as they see visible evidence of their progress and are motivated to improve their rate and accuracy. The charts can be a meaningful way to gather evidence of fluency development over time with a variety of passages. As a chart is completed for a passage, it can be placed in the student's work folder or portfolio.

### ◆◆◆ EVALUATION (student behaviors to look for) ◆◆◆

✦ Decrease in miscues as noted on the Reading Progress Chart

✦ Increase in speed or rate as noted on the Reading Progress Chart

✦ Appropriate expression

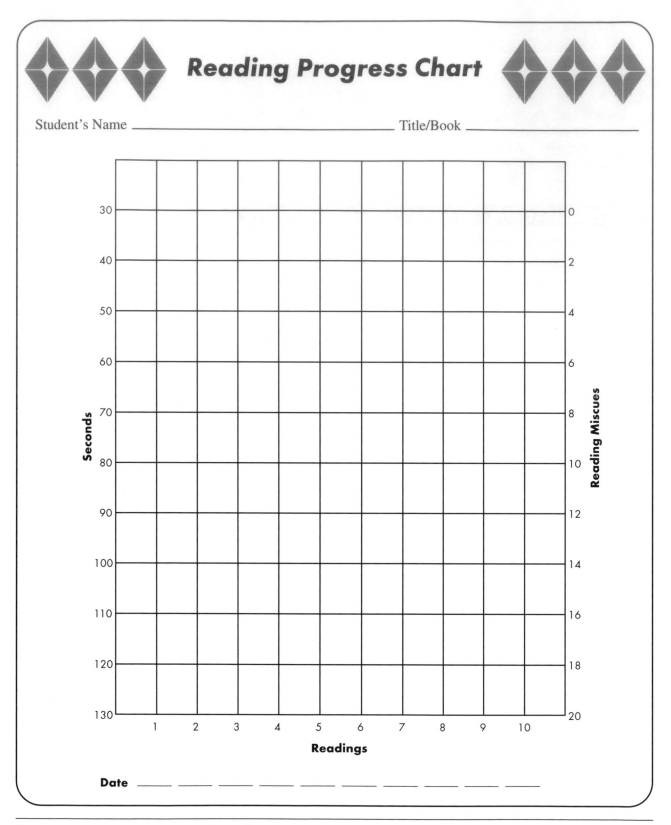

## Reading Progress Chart

Student's Name _____ Title/Book _____

**Seconds** (left axis): 30, 40, 50, 60, 70, 80, 90, 100, 110, 120, 130

**Reading Miscues** (right axis): 0, 2, 4, 6, 8, 10, 12, 14, 16, 18, 20

**Readings** (bottom axis): 1, 2, 3, 4, 5, 6, 7, 8, 9, 10

**Date** _____ _____ _____ _____ _____ _____ _____ _____ _____ _____

# Simplified Repeated Reading

## MATERIALS

✧ Reading selections

## USE

✧ Partner

## DESCRIPTION

The method of Structured Repeated Reading (see page 69) was first introduced over 25 years ago (Samuels, 1979). Recently, Samuels (2002) simplified the method so that it does not require charting or computation of reading speed. In addition, after training, students can use it independently with minimal assistance from the teacher. Samuels recommends that Simplified Repeated Reading "should be used with students who are not yet automatic at word recognition, usually first and second graders" (Samuels, 2002, p. 178). This strategy is very similar to the Fluency Development Lesson (see page 54).

## PROCEDURE

1. Ask students how one becomes skilled in sports or some other activity with which students can relate. Guide the discussion as necessary so students realize that practice and repetition are key elements of becoming skilled. Then relate the process to reading.

2. Select appropriate materials for students to use. These materials can be from instructional materials or the classroom library.

3. Read the selected passage to the class while students follow along silently.

4. Assign each student to a partner. If possible, pair a better reader with a poorer reader. Once the reading begins, students will work on their own in pairs.

5. Have one student of the pair take the role of the teacher, and the other take the role of the student. Explain that the role of the student is to read the passage orally. The role of the teacher is to listen to oral reading while looking at the words in the text. This procedure allows both students to get practice with the passage. Model the process with a student if necessary.

6. Following the first reading, have students reverse roles and read. Then reverse roles and repeat the process. Repeat the process again so each passage is read four times.

7. Repeat the above process for each daily session. Samuels notes that "most of the gains in reading speed, word recognition error reduction, and expression in oral reading are acquired by the fourth reading" (Samuels, 2002, p. 178). He bases his statement on research by O'Shea, Sindelar, and O'Shea (1985).

## EVALUATION (student behaviors to look for)

✧ Increase in accuracy in word identification

✧ Increase in speed or rate

✧ Appropriate expression

# Student Self-Managed Repeated Reading

## ◇◈◇ MATERIALS ▶◆◆

◇ Typed copies of passages near students' independent reading levels, with word counts determined and noted

◇ Books or materials containing the original passages (optional)

◇ Stopwatches

◇ Calculators

◇ Pencils in various colors

◇ Folders and copies of the Untimed Repeated Reading Record Sheet and the Timed Repeated Reading Record Sheet reproducibles (pages 78–79)

◇ Student folders for completed Reading Record Sheets

◇ Tape recorders and cassette tapes (optional)

## ◇◈◇ USE ▶◆◆

◇ Partner

## ◇◈◇ DESCRIPTION ▶◆◆◆ ◆◆◆◆◆◆◆◆◆◆◆◆◆◆◆◆◆◆◆◆◆◆◆

In this modified method of Repeated Reading (Samuels, 1979), student partners manage their own fluency development. Through modeling and scaffolding provided by the teacher, students are taught to note miscues and rate, calculate words correct per minute (WCPM), and complete record sheets of their progress (Moskal, 2005/2006). In addition to improving students' fluency, this approach can also increase students' self-efficacy and confidence, thereby motivating them to achieve reading success.

## ✦✦✦ PROCEDURE ▸◆◆

1. Before students can successfully participate in the activity independently, it is necessary to engage them in several modeling and practice sessions lasting from 30–45 minutes each. Sessions include the components suggested by Johnson, Graham, and Harris (1997).

   ✧ Show students the techniques required for conducting repeated readings of text—gathering necessary materials, reading passages orally, completing a mini-miscue analysis, calculating words correct per minute (WCPM), completing the Record Sheets, and putting materials away.

   ✧ Begin by teaching students how to complete a mini-miscue analysis by misreading a passage of 20–30 words aloud to students, having them underline the miscues, and then discussing them. Note how miscues affect fluent reading.

   ✧ Model how to track rate using a stopwatch and determine words correct per minute using a calculator.

   ✧ Teach students how to complete each of the Record Sheets on pages 78–79.

   ✧ During guided reading practice sessions, or in small group instruction, allow students to work in pairs to practice several of the Repeated Reading activities. Closely observe students and offer assistance as needed.

   ✧ Students may need up to fifteen practice sessions before they can successfully complete all aspects of the Repeated Reading activity independently (Moskal, 2005/2006).

2. When you believe that students are ready to engage in the activity successfully, establish a designated area in your classroom for students to conduct Repeated Readings. Make sure that all necessary materials are readily accessible to students.

3. Select passages from materials that you have used in small group guided reading lessons and that are close to students' independent reading levels.

4. Assign student partners by selecting students who can work independently and have strong word recognition skills and fluency rates close to their grade level.

5. Have student pairs meet at the designated area. When both partners are ready, one student reads the typed copy or the material containing the original passage aloud while the listener carefully follows along with a copy of the same text. If the reader makes an error, the listener underlines the misread word using a colored pencil.

6. At the completion of the reading, the student listener asks the reader questions from the Untimed Repeated Reading Record Sheet (see page 78).

7. The reader then completes the self-assessment section of the Untimed Repeated Reading Record Sheet, records the number of miscues, and sets a fluency goal for the next reading of the passage.

8. Student pairs repeat the process, the listener recording miscues using a different colored pencil.

9. Following the second reading and recording, student partners switch roles. Then the entire process is repeated.

10. At the conclusion of the session, students file their completed Record Sheets in the designated folders.

11. Students can repeat the process up to five times using the same passage. During the final session, the listener can time the reading and record the words correct per minute (WCPM) on the Timed Repeated Reading Record Sheet (page 79).

## ✧✦✧ EVALUATION *(student behaviors to look for)* ▸◆◆

✧ Increase in accuracy in word identification

✧ Increase in rate

✧ Appropriate expression

✧ Improvement in the items listed on the Untimed and Timed Repeated Reading Record Sheets

# Untimed Repeated Reading Record

# Fluency Record

Name _____ Date _____

Title _____ Start Page _____ End Page _____

## First Reading
How do you think you read? _____

How can your partner help you? _____
Did you understand what you read?   Yes   No   (If no, can your partner help?)

Number of Miscues _____

| I used the punctuation correctly. | Almost Always | Sometimes | Rarely |
| I read with expression. | Almost Always | Sometimes | Rarely |
| I was able to read smoothly, without pausing a lot. | Almost Always | Sometimes | Rarely |
| The reading sounded like talking. | Almost Always | Sometimes | Rarely |

Goal for next reading (circle one above)

## Second Reading
How do you think you read? _____

How can your partner help you? _____
Did you understand what you read?   Yes   No   (If no, can your partner help?)

Number of Miscues _____

| I used the punctuation correctly. | Almost Always | Sometimes | Rarely |
| I read with expression. | Almost Always | Sometimes | Rarely |
| I was able to read smoothly, without pausing a lot. | Almost Always | Sometimes | Rarely |
| The reading sounded like talking. | Almost Always | Sometimes | Rarely |

I was able to reach my goal.   Yes   No

My goal for the next reading is _____

Adapted from Moskal, M.K. (2005/2006). Student self-selected repeated reading: Successful fluency development for disfluent readers. *Illinois Reading Council Journal, 34*(1), 3–11.

# Timed Reading Record

Name _____   Date _____

Title _____   Level _____

Start Page _____ End Page _____ Number of Words _____

**First Reading**

Number of Miscues _____   Number of Seconds _____

_____ words − _____ miscues = _____ ÷ _____ seconds × 60 = [ ] WCPM

| | | | |
|---|---|---|---|
| I used the punctuation correctly. | Almost Always | Sometimes | Rarely |
| I read with expression. | Almost Always | Sometimes | Rarely |
| I was able to group words that went together. | Almost Always | Sometimes | Rarely |
| The reading sounded like talking. | Almost Always | Sometimes | Rarely |

WCPM goal for the next reading [ ]

**Second Reading**

Number of Miscues _____   Number of Seconds _____

_____ words − _____ miscues = _____ ÷ _____ seconds × 60 = [ ] WCPM

| | | | |
|---|---|---|---|
| I used the punctuation correctly. | Almost Always | Sometimes | Rarely |
| I read with expression. | Almost Always | Sometimes | Rarely |
| I was able to group words that went together. | Almost Always | Sometimes | Rarely |
| The reading sounded like talking. | Almost Always | Sometimes | Rarely |

Did you reach your goal?   Yes   No      WCPM goal for the next reading [ ]

I still need to work on _____

Adapted from Moskal, M.K. (2005/2006). Student self-selected repeated reading: Sucessful fluency development for disfluent readers. *Illinois Reading Council Journal, 34*(1), 3–11.

# Tape, Check, Chart

## MATERIALS

✧ Reading selection
✧ Copy of reading selection
✧ Tape Recorder
✧ Three different colored pens, pencils, or markers
✧ Tape, Check, Chart reproducible for each student (page 82)

## USE

✧ Individual

## DESCRIPTION

In this adaptation of repeated readings, students listen to audiotapes of their own reading and record their miscues. According to Allington (2001), the number of miscues generally decreases with each reading and fluency increases. In addition, having students note and chart their own progress is a visible record of their improvement and serves as an incentive to continue to work toward greater fluency.

## ⬡⬡⬡ PROCEDURE ▸◆◆

1. Have the student read aloud a text of appropriate difficulty and record it on an audiotape. An appropriate text for repeated readings is one that the student can read with at least 90% accuracy.

2. After making the recording, have the student replay the tape and follow along in the text (or with a photocopy of the text).

3. As he or she listens to the tape recording, the student places a small check mark above each word that deviates from the text (e.g., omissions, insertions, mispronunciations).

4. Then have the student read and make another recording of the same passage. The student again notes, in a second color, any omissions, insertions, or mispronunciations with a check mark.

5. The student reads the same passage a third time, tapes the reading, listens again to the tape and marks, in a third color, the deviations from text.

6. The student should tally and chart the number of text deviations for each reading, using the chart on page 82.

7. Meet with the student to discuss his or her progress. Give recognition for effort and progress.

## ⬡⬡⬡ EVALUATION (student behaviors to look for) ▸◆◆

✧ Reduction of miscues on the Tape, Check, Chart reproducible

✧ Ability to monitor taped reading

✧ Self-perceptions of improvement

 # Tape, Check, Chart

Name _____ Date _____

Passage _____

| RECORDING NUMBER | NUMBER OF CHECK MARKS (✓) | COMMENTS |
|---|---|---|
| 1 | | |
| 2 | | |
| 3 | | |

Name _____ Date _____

Passage _____

| RECORDING NUMBER | NUMBER OF CHECK MARKS (✓) | COMMENTS |
|---|---|---|
| 1 | | |
| 2 | | |
| 3 | | |

Name _____ Date _____

Passage _____

| RECORDING NUMBER | NUMBER OF CHECK MARKS (✓) | COMMENTS |
|---|---|---|
| 1 | | |
| 2 | | |
| 3 | | |

FLUENCY GOALS

COMPREHENSION

ACCURACY

EXPRESSION

SPEED

# Reading While Listening

## ⬥⬥⬥ MATERIALS ⬥⬥⬥

✧ Text selection for each student

✧ Text recordings of the reading selections

✧ Tape recorder and headphones

✧ Reading While Listening Progress Chart reproducible for each student (page 86)

## ⬥⬥⬥ USE ⬥⬥⬥

✧ Individual

✧ Small Group

## ⬥⬥⬥ DESCRIPTION ⬥⬥⬥ ⬥⬥⬥⬥⬥⬥⬥⬥⬥⬥⬥⬥⬥⬥⬥⬥⬥

In Reading While Listening (or repeated listening), students listen to recorded passages while they silently read the written version (Kuhn & Stahl, 2000). Texts with tapes or CD-ROMs are available commercially; however, in order to make the experience the most valuable, the recorded texts need to be at the students' instructional level and recorded at a speed that enables them to follow along. Cues need to be explicit (e.g., when to turn pages) to minimize students losing their places. Also, reading in phrases and having students slide their fingers under the words helps students to stay on task (Carbo, 1978, 1981). Having the teacher, teaching assistant, or parent helper prepare recordings provides the optimal opportunity for students to gain from the experience. Students who become familiar with the procedure and are fairly fluent readers can also create recordings for classroom use (Rasinski & Padak, 1996). The advantage of Reading While Listening over Structured Repeated Reading (see page 69) or the Neurological Impress Method (see page 64) is that there is much less assistance needed from the teacher, because the modeling of fluent reading is provided by the recording. This makes the procedure more usable in a classroom situation. Holding students accountable for being able to read the text fluently at the completion of several Reading While Listening sessions is critical to the success of this activity. Students know that they must practice the materials repeatedly, in order to meet the success criterion. Dowhower (1987) and Rasinski (1990) found that students made significant gains in reading speed and accuracy, and students in Carbo's study (1981) demonstrated gains in word recognition. In fact, Rasinski's study (1990) and one by Sindelar, Monda, and O'Shea (1990) found that Reading While Listening is effective for students with learning disabilities, as well as for students who represent both the the low-success and high-success range of readers in the classroom. Kuhn and Stahl (2000) caution that it is important to make a distinction between Reading While Listening and classroom listening centers. Classroom listening center experiences generally don't include holding students responsible for reading the material in a fluent manner after repeated listening experiences; therefore, students don't practice reading the material, and as a result, do not appear to make measurable gains in reading.

## PROCEDURE

1. Select materials that are of interest to students and that are challenging, but not at the students' frustration level.

2. Prepare recordings of the materials, using the following guidelines:

    ✧ Read aloud at a comfortable rate, so that students can follow along.

    ✧ Read with good phrasing and expression.

    ✧ Give oral or auditory signal cues to students when a page should be turned.

    ✧ If page lay-out makes it difficult for students to know where the reading will begin, tell them explicitly on the recording where to look when following along.

    ✧ You may wish to encourage students to finger-point to the words as they listen or use an index card or paper marker to help them keep their places.

3. Provide several copies of the text so that a small group of students may participate in the activity simultaneously. See the suggested resources on the following page.

4. Tell students that they are going to be listening to material that they will be expected to read aloud to you at a future date. Tell them that, after listening and following along several times, you will expect them to be able to read with expression, accuracy, and at a rate that sounds like they are talking.

5. Following the listening, have students practice reading the material several more times either independently and/or with a partner.

6. Finally, provide an opportunity for students to read the material aloud to you, an older student, a teaching assistant, or parent volunteer.

7. Track students' progress, paying particular attention to accuracy and rate (see Reading While Listening Progress Chart on page 86).

## EVALUATION (student behaviors to look for)

✧ Active engagement

✧ Improvement in items listed on the Reading While Listening Progress Chart

*High five reading.* Mankato, MN: Red Brick Learning
(www.redbricklearning.com) 888-262-6135

This is a series of 15 nonfiction books and audiocassette tapes for students in the primary and intermediate grades. The books are written on a variety of reading levels and cover a range of interest areas, including biography, sports, adventure, science, and history. The audio tapes are recorded at two speeds to enable students to listen at a rate that is comfortable for them.

Soliloquy Learning, Union City, CA
(www.soliloquylearning.com) 866-442-0920

This publisher, with the guidance of Marilyn Jager Adams, has created the Soliloquy Reading Assistant (available at www.reading-assistant.com). The CD rom uses advanced speech recognition software to provide feedback to students as they practice repeated oral readings. The most innovative feature of these materials is that the rate of reading is determined by the student rather than the software, thus enhancing the potential for fluency improvement. Reading selections are drawn from such sources as *Cricket* and *Spider* magazines and are appropriate for students in grades two through five.

Sundance Publishers, Littleton, MA
(www.sundancepub.com) 800-343-8204

This publisher has many recorded books that are unabridged sources for student listening and reading. Here are a few possibilities:

Fritz, J. *Stories of famous Americans.* Books and Cassettes (Grades 3–6)
Rey, H. A. *Curious George.* Books and Cassettes (Grades K–3)
Lobel, A. *Frog and Toad.* Books and Cassettes (Grades K–3)
Rylant, C. *Henry and Mudge.* Books and Cassettes (Grades K–3)
*People to remember.* Read-Along Cassettes (Grades 3 and up)

*Some additional titles of talking books follow:*

Dr. Seuss's ABC (1995). Living Books series. Novato, CA: Random House—Broderbund Software.
Tronic Phonics (1997). New York: Macmillan/McGraw-Hill Software.

# Reading While Listening Progress Chart

Name _____

Title of Selection _____ Level _____

| FOCUS | 1 | 2 | 3 | 4 |
|---|---|---|---|---|
| **Rate** | Slow and laborious Struggles with words | Rate varies Some hesitations | Generally conversational Some smooth, some choppy | Conversational and consistent Smooth and fluent throughout |
| **Expression** | Monotone | Monotone combined with some expression | Appropriate expression used much of the time | Appropriate expression maintained throughout |
| **Phrasing** | Word-by-word Long pauses between words | Some word-by-word, some phrases | Mostly phrases, some smooth, some choppy | Phrases consistently throughout, generally smooth and fluent |
| **Punctuation** | Little or no use | Uses some Ignores some | Uses most of the time | Uses consistently throughout |

| READING | DATE | TIME (IN SECONDS) | NUMBER OF MISCUES COUNTED AS ERRORS | HOLISTIC SCORE (CIRCLE A RATING IN EACH FOCUS AREA ABOVE AND ADD THE SCORES) |
|---|---|---|---|---|
| 1 | | | | |
| 2 | | | | |
| 3 | | | | |

From Jerry L. Johns and Roberta L. Berglund, *Fluency: Strategies & Assessments* (3rd ed.). Copyright © 2006 Kendall/Hunt Publishing Company (1-800-247-3458, ext. 4 or 5). May be reproduced for noncommercial educational purposes.

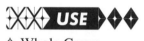

# Klassroom Karaoke

✧ Karaoke machine

✧ Television

✧ Cables for video and audio

✧ Compact discs with graphics (CDGs)

✧ Microphone (optional)

✧ Copies of the song lyrics for each student

**USE** ◆◆

✧ Whole Group

**DESCRIPTION** ◆◆◆ ◆◆◆◆◆◆◆◆◆◆◆◆◆◆◆◆◆◆◆◆◆◆◆◆◆

Karaoke is the singing of songs using a recording without the lead vocals. Using karaoke helps students to build reading fluency through music. Children's songs and traditional folk songs are good choices for karaoke activities. Karaoke machines use compact discs with graphics (CDGs). There are many CDGs available, some in languages other than English. This feature makes them especially useful in bilingual classrooms. When the karaoke machine is connected to a television, the CDG shows the words on the television screen. CDGs vary in their audio format. Some have only the instrumental track while others include the vocal tracks as well. The CDGs which include the vocal tracks are best for learning a new song or remembering the verses when only the chorus can be recalled.

**PROCEDURE** ◆◆

1. Set up the necessary equipment, including a karaoke machine, television, cables for video and audio, and CDGs. Microphones are optional. Make sure that all equipment is working before beginning the lesson.

2. Select a few of your favorite songs to teach the students. Begin with one song.

3. Play the song with the vocal track while students follow along silently with the words on the television screen.

4. Play the song again and pause the karaoke machine so students can read each screen aloud.

5. Play the song a third time and encourage the students to sing along with the vocals in unison.

6. In repeated experiences, students can then sing as a group, in trios, pairs, or solo.

7. If you choose to use the microphone, show students how it works. Some karaoke machines block out the CDG vocals when the microphone is used.

8. Copy the text of the song for students to use in repeated readings. An adaptation might be to create the text in a cloze version, leaving out some of the vocabulary words, idioms, phrases, or English language structures. This adaptation is particularly useful for English Language Learners.

9. When students are comfortable with both the music and words, play the song without the vocal track and encourage students to sing along with the accompaniment.

10. After many opportunities for practice with supports, some students may wish to write the lyrics from memory. They can check their work for accuracy with the karaoke machine.

## ✠✠✠ EVALUATION (student behaviors to look for) ▸◆◆

✧ Accuracy of word identification

✧ Ability to follow along with words and music

✧ Appropriate expression

Thanks are extended to Ana Schmitz Viveros, a teacher of English Language Learners from Minneapolis, MN, for sharing this idea.

# Performance Reading

# Say It Like the Character

**MATERIALS**

✧ Reading selection
✧ Sentence strips
✧ Emotion cards

**USE**

✧ Whole Group
✧ Small Group

**DESCRIPTION**

Say It Like the Character helps students learn to make inferences as they become more fluent readers (Opitz & Rasinski, 1998). When students read silently, they may not think about the way a character feels or how the character might speak. In Say It Like the Character, students are developing prosody as they are asked to read aloud using the intonation and expression they believe the character in the story might use when speaking. Thus, the story becomes more meaningful, and interpretations about the character are elicited.

**PROCEDURE**

1. Ask students to read a given text silently. Be sure the selection contains character dialogue.

2. Select a segment of the text and ask students to reread it silently, thinking about how the character(s) might sound when speaking.

3. Invite a student or students to read the segment aloud in the way the character(s) might actually speak, thus conveying the feelings of the character(s) to the listener. You might use some of the following questions:

    ✧ What emotion(s) were you conveying as you read to us?

    ✧ What made you decide to read as you did?

    ✧ Did you connect something in your own experience with that of the character(s)? If so, what?

    ✧ Were there any typographic signals in the text that helped you know how to use your voice, for instance, large, bold type or exclamation marks?

4. As students continue reading silently, encourage them to pay attention to the events in the story, the typographical signals the author gives, and the ways the author helps the reader understand the characters and their feelings.

5. As a follow-up activity, you may wish to do the following:

⬥ Have students share the signals in the selection that they used to "say it like the character."

⬥ Select sentences from the text and print them on sentence strips. For example,

"What is that crazy horse doing?" people asked one another.

The ducks marched right out of the park in a straight line.

Night came, and the lights went on in the city.

"But wait! We need to get the camera."

Waving his arms frantically, he shouted at the driver to stop.

We worked side by side . . . long into the night.

"Dress warmly, Jenny," her mom called.

She swallowed hard, "I've learned a lot this summer."

⬥ Print words that convey specific emotions on index cards. Some example words might be *fear, excitement, joy,* and *anger.*

⬥ Invite students to choose one emotion card and one sentence strip and then read the sentence aloud, conveying the emotion on the card. Listeners might be invited to guess the emotion being expressed by the reader, thus turning it into a game and enhancing motivation for fluency practice (Person, 1993). See Guess the Emotion on page 92.

## EVALUATION (student behaviors to look for)

⬥ Making appropriate inferences about character emotions

⬥ Appropriate expression

# Guess the Emotion

 **MATERIALS** ◆◆

✧ Sentence strips
✧ Emotion cards

**USE** ◆◆

✧ Small Group

**DESCRIPTION** ◆◆◆◆◆◆◆◆◆◆◆◆◆◆◆◆◆◆◆◆◆◆◆◆◆◆◆◆

Guess the Emotion provides students with an opportunity to read brief sentences using their voices to convey a feeling. Their classmates, in turn, try to guess the emotion being expressed. This small-group activity is a pleasurable way for students to develop aspects of prosody: intonation, phrasing, voice quality, and attention to punctuation.

**PROCEDURE** ◆◆

1. Make a set of sentence strips for each small group of 5–7 students. Use the suggested sentences on page 94 or choose some from materials available in your school.

2. Prepare a set of emotion cards for each group (see pages 95–96). You may use the ones provided or create your own. You may wish to reproduce the emotion cards on card stock and laminate them for multiple uses.

3. Have students get into small groups. They can sit on the floor or around tables.

4. Place the sentence strips and emotion cards in two piles face down in the center of the group.

5. Begin by having one student draw a sentence strip from the pile. The student should first read the sentence silently and then orally for initial practice. If the student has difficulty with any of the words in the sentence, the student may ask for assistance from another member of the group.

6. Next, the same student draws an emotion card from the pile. The card is not shown to the rest of the group. The student rereads the sentence aloud using the expression or emotion indicated on the card. (If the expression/emotion card simply does not fit the sentence, the student may draw another card.)

7. Students in the group then guess which emotion the reader is conveying. You may wish to provide a list of emotions for students to consult.

8. When the emotion is guessed or told by the reader, the next student takes a turn until all in the group have had an opportunity to participate.

9. A variation of this activity is to provide the same sentence to all the students and have them draw different emotion cards. This variation conveys the ways the meaning of a sentence changes depending on the way it is read aloud.

## ◆◆◆ EVALUATION (student behaviors to look for) ▶◆◆

✧ Communicating "emotional" meaning

✧ Appropriate intonation, phrasing, voice quality, and attention to punctuation

Thanks are extended to Susan Bolek, Maryanne Dihel, and Judy Martus, Community Consolidated School District 93, Carol Stream, IL for sharing this idea.

# Sample Sentence Strips

1. The queen said, "Let them eat cake."

2. The handsome prince said, "I will kill the dragon and win the hand of the fair princess."

3. The coach said, "I am a strong person, but he is stronger and smarter."

4. The lightning flashed! Dracula said, "The castle is cold tonight, my dear. I think we need a fire."

5. Betty said, "I am afraid of the dark."

6. Dr. Frankenstein's monster said, "Don't be afraid. I won't hurt you."

7. The burglar said, "Your money or your life."

8. Snow White said, "I hope that the seven dwarfs will be home soon. They are very late tonight."

9. The king said, "It is a cold day. Bring me my fur robe."

10. The mother said, "You are the nicest child in the whole world."

11. Superman said, "I must save the world from the evil Captain Crazy. He wants to destroy the city."

12. The teacher said, "Children, you must finish your homework tonight. There will be a test tomorrow."

13. Dad said, "Go upstairs and get your homework done right now."

14. Lance Armstrong said, "This is the greatest bike race in the world."

From Jerry L. Johns and Roberta L. Berglund, *Fluency: Strategies & Assessments* (3rd ed.). Copyright © 2006 Kendall/Hunt Publishing Company (1-800-247-3458, ext. 4 or 5). May be reproduced for noncommercial educational purposes.

| | |
|---|---|
| scared | *Sweet* |
| Excited | **ANGRY** |
| Happy | *Sad* |
| BORED | CONFUSED |
| SURPRISED | CONFIDENT |

From Jerry L. Johns and Roberta L. Berglund, *Fluency: Strategies & Assessments* (3rd ed.). Copyright © 2006 Kendall/Hunt Publishing Company (1-800-247-3458, ext. 4 or 5). May be reproduced for noncommercial educational purposes.

| | |
|---|---|
| **BRAVE** | Silly |
| Nervous | **Threatening** |
| | |
| | |
| | |

# Readers Theater

✧ Readers Theater script for each student

✧ Whole Group
✧ Small Group

### ◇◇◇ DESCRIPTION ◇◇◇ ◆◆◆◆◆◆◆◆◆◆◆◆◆◆◆◆◆◆◆◆◆◆◆◆

Readers Theater is a viable vehicle for oral reading fluency (Keehn, 2003) and a genuine way to promote repeated readings (Rasinski, 2000). It is a presentation of text read aloud expressively and dramatically by two or more readers (Young & Vardell, 1993). Meaning is conveyed to the audience, primarily through readers' expressive and interpretive readings rather than through actions, costumes, or props. Students can read from commercially-prepared scripts or develop scripts from materials they are reading, either narrative or expository in nature. General characteristics of Readers Theater include: no full memorization; holding scripts during the performance; no full costumes or staging; and narration providing a framework for the dramatic action conveyed by the readers. The primary aim of Readers Theater is to promote reading (Shepard, 1997), and it appears to do so, as the practice for a Readers Theater performance gives new purpose and added enjoyment for reading stories and books repeatedly. Martinez, Roser, and Strecker (1998/1999) offered an instructional plan for developing Readers Theater with young readers using narrative text, and Roser (2001) demonstrated that Readers Theater strategies can also help Hispanic middle-grade students learn to read in their second language of English. Flynn (2004/2005) suggested that having students write and perform scripts based on curriculum materials involves students in demonstrating comprehension, summarizing, synthesizing, and communicating information.

## PROCEDURE ◆◆

1. Develop or select a script to be used with students. Such development may mean adding brief narration to describe the action in the story or dividing longer narrations into speaking parts for more than one narrator. Possible resources are listed below.

2. Read aloud from the story on which the script is based. Provide a good model of fluent reading.

3. Provide a brief lesson on one aspect of fluency, perhaps noting the signals in the text that might help students know how to read it aloud, or discuss how the characters might be feeling at selected points in the story. This discussion should help provide insights about how each character might sound.

4. Distribute scripts to the students and have them read silently or with a buddy. You may want to encourage students to take the scripts home for additional practice.

5. The next day, have students practice reading the script aloud again; then determine who will be reading each role for performance purposes.

6. Have students spend the next day highlighting their parts in the script and reading and rereading their assigned roles with their group. Encourage students to think about how they might best convey the feelings of the character they are representing. They should also consider other ways they can help the audience understand the story and where they will stand or sit during the performance.

7. Finally, in front of an audience consisting of parents, school personnel, or other members of the class, have students perform their Readers Theater production.

8. Possible resources for Readers Theater scripts are listed below.

## EVALUATION (student behaviors to look for) ◆◆

✧ Evidence of textual understanding through the use of appropriate gestures, facial expressions, and voice
✧ Accuracy of word identification
✧ Appropriate rate
✧ Appropriate intonation, phrasing, voice quality, and attention to punctuation

## SUGGESTED RESOURCES ◆◆
### for Readers Theater

http://www.aaronshep.com/rt
http://www.poetryteachers.com
http://www.readerstheatre.ecsd.net
http://readinglady.com
http://scriptsforschools.com
http://www.cdli.ca/CITE/langrt.htm
http://www.storycart.com
Barchers, S. I. (1993). *Readers theatre for beginning readers*. Portsmouth, NH: Teacher Ideas Press.
Bauer, C. F. (1991). *Presenting reader's theater: Plays and poems to read aloud*. New York: H. W. Wilson.
Braun, W., & Braun, C. (2000). *A readers theatre treasury of stories*. Calgary: Braun & Braun.
Dixon, N., Davies, A., & Politano, C. (1996). *Learning with readers theatre*. Winnipeg, MB: Peguis.

Fredericks, A. (1993). *Frantic frogs and other frankly fractured folktales for readers theatre.* Portsmouth, NH: Teacher Ideas Press.

Fredericks, A. (1997). *Tadpole tales and other totally terrific treats for readers theatre.* Portsmouth, NH: Teacher Ideas Press.

Fredericks, A. (2000). *Silly salamanders and other slightly stupid stuff for readers theatre.* Portsmouth, NH: Teacher Ideas Press.

Glasscock, S. (2000). *10 American history plays for the classroom.* New York: Scholastic.

Haven, K. (1996). *Great moments in science experiments and readers theatre.* Portsmouth, NH: Teacher Ideas Press.

Ratliff, G.L. (1999). *Introduction to readers theatre: A classroom guide to performance.* Colorado Springs, CO: Meriwether Publishing.

Shepard, A. (2004). *Folktales on stage: Children's plays for reader's theater.* Redondo Beach, CA: Shepard.

Sloyer, S. (2003). *From the page to the stage: The educator's complete guide to readers theatre.* Westport, CT: Teacher Ideas Press.

Walker, L. (1997). *Readers theatre strategies for the middle and junior high classroom.* Colorado Springs, CO: Meriwether Publishing.

# Independent Reading

# Read and Relax

**MATERIALS**

✧ Reading selections

✧ Rules for Read and Relax reproducible for each student (page 104) (optional)

**USE**

✧ Whole Group

**DESCRIPTION**

Read and Relax is an adaptation of Sustained Silent Reading (see page 105) developed for use in primary-grade classrooms (Maro, 2001, 2004). Similar to Sustained Silent Reading, all students read silently for a given amount of time each day. One major difference between Sustained Silent Reading and Read and Relax is that Read and Relax requires students to read materials that are at their independent reading levels—text that can be read with 99% accuracy in word recognition and 90% comprehension (Betts, 1946; Johns, 2005a). Another difference is that the teacher uses think-alouds to help students understand how to select materials and use metacognitive comprehension strategies when reading independently. Also in Read and Relax, the teacher monitors students' reading by asking students to read portions of the text aloud to the teacher. The opportunity for students to self-select materials and read them for an uninterrupted period of time increases the number of words read and also increases students' involvement in the reading process. Through the process of reading many easy books, students become more fluent readers and gain competence and confidence (Gillet, Temple, & Crawford, 2004).

**PROCEDURE**

1. A well-supplied classroom library that contains materials at a wide variety of levels is essential to Read and Relax.

2. Gather a few books from the classroom library and model a Read and Relax session for your students. Gather students around you and explain that you are going to show them what Read and Relax looks

like so that they will know what to do when it is their turn to Read and Relax. Explain to students that they will read their selections silently.

3. Open your first book and make a prediction about its content. Begin to read aloud and reflect on your predictions, making your thinking apparent to your students. Continue to read aloud, sharing your reading and your thinking as you read. You may want to show students how you ask questions and make connections as you read. For example, when reading a book about cats, you might say, "My cat falls asleep after she eats, just like the cat in this story. I wonder if cats need a special place to sleep or if they just fall asleep anywhere. Maybe I will find out as I continue to read this book."

4. In order to demonstrate what to do when a book is too difficult, struggle with some words in one of your Read and Relax books. After struggling with several words, tell your students that you can't relax with this book; therefore, it is too difficult for your Read and Relax time. Put it down and begin to read another book, modeling fluent reading. Explain that with an easy book, you can say almost all of the words and understand the story. Tell students that they should read easy books during their Read and Relax time, books that they can read comfortably.

5. On another day, invite students to select books and get ready for Read and Relax time. Remind them of the rules for Read and Relax, such as no talking to other students and always having several books ready to read. You may wish to post the rules so students can refer to them as needed.

6. Once Read and Relax has begun and students appear to be able to follow the behavioral guidelines, you may then begin to monitor students as they are reading. Quietly stop by students' desks and ask individual students to read some of their books to you. If the student is struggling when reading and doesn't sound relaxed, encourage the student to find an easier, more suitable, text. You might say, "You are working too hard. Find a book that you will feel more relaxed reading."

## ✛✕✕✦ EVALUATION (student behaviors to look for) ▸◆◆

✧ Improvement in items listed on the Rules for Read and Relax reproducible

✧ Rate indicating that the materials are "just right" for the student

✧ Appropriate text-related comments and questions

✧ Increased confidence in reading selected materials

# Rules for Read and Relax

- ✧ Find books that are easy for you to read by yourself, books that you can read comfortably.

- ✧ Have your books ready for Read and Relax time.

- ✧ If you need to, get a drink and go to the bathroom before Read and Relax begins.

- ✧ Keep your hands and feet to yourself.

- ✧ Keep reading. Stop only when your teacher tells you to.

- ✧ Stay quiet.

# Sustained Silent Reading (SSR)

 **MATERIALS**

◇ Reading selections

◇ Sharing Your Reading reproducible for each student (page 107)

◇ Rules for SSR Time reproducible for each student (page 108) (optional)

 **USE**

◇ Whole Group

**DESCRIPTION**

Sustained Silent Reading (SSR) encourages students to practice reading self-selected materials, during a designated time in the school day (Berglund & Johns, 1983; Hunt, 1970). The purpose is to provide an opportunity for students to develop fluency and, at the same time, expand their vocabulary, and comprehension abilities, develop broader knowledge of written language, and provide a powerful source for world knowledge (Gillet, Temple, & Crawford, 2004). Allington (1983b) found that students do very little reading outside of school. This contributes to Stanovich's "Matthew effects" (1986), which suggests that those who read more tend to continue to become better readers, while those who read less, especially poorer readers, tend not to choose to read and, therefore, fall farther and farther behind. Sustained Silent Reading provides an opportunity for all students to build fluency in their reading through regular opportunities to practice (Pearson & Fielding, 1991). Successful reading practice develops rapid, flexible word identification skills and strategies, builds vocabulary, and contributes to overall reading achievement.

## PROCEDURE ▶◆◆

1. Tell students that they will be having an opportunity to choose something that they would like to read and to read it for a specified period of time. Provide an opportunity for students to locate the materials and have them ready for the SSR period.

2. Designate a specific time during the day when all students will participate in SSR. Some teachers choose to do this during reading workshop or during self-selected reading time, if they are using the four-block model (Cunningham, 1999.)

3. Go over the procedures and guidelines so that students understand expectations during this time. See page 108 for some suggested Rules for SSR Time, adapted from Anderson (2000). A useful handbook for organizing and managing an SSR program has been prepared by Pilgreen (2000).

4. Start with a short period of time, especially for young or less able students. Expand the time as students appear ready. When students ask if they can continue reading after the time is up, consider that a signal to increase your SSR time.

5. Provide materials for students who can't find something to read or who run short of materials before the time is up.

6. Be a model of good reading yourself. Students will be interested in what you are reading and will grow to understand that adults, as well as students, choose to read for pleasure, both in and out of school. (Some teachers choose to balance modeling reading with conferring with their students about their reading. At least two days a week they read during SSR and on the other days, they confer with their students.)

7. Following the SSR period, compliment students on their behavior and their consideration of others during the reading time. You also may invite students to comment on their reading, if they wish. Comments may lead to extended enjoyment and to spontaneous sharing of text segments, thus promoting meaningful and positive practice in fluency and creating desire in others to read the same materials at another time. A few students may be offered a more extensive opportunity to tell about their reading (3 minutes) and persuade others in the class to read the same materials. (See the Sharing Your Reading chart on the following page.)

## EVALUATION (student behaviors to look for) ▶◆◆

✧ Improvement in items listed on the Sharing Your Reading reproducible
✧ Improvement in items listed on the Rules for SSR Time reproducible
✧ Rate indicating that the materials are of an appropriate level of difficulty for the student
✧ Increased confidence in reading selected materials

# Sharing Your Reading

✧ You have a maximum of three minutes to tell the group about your reading today.

✧ If you read fiction, you must include:

> ✧ title
> ✧ author
> ✧ where it took place (setting)
> ✧ the main characters
> ✧ one part that you liked best

✧ If you read for information, you must include:

> ✧ title
> ✧ author
> ✧ what the reading was mostly about
> ✧ one thing that you learned or found interesting from your reading

✧ Tell us if you would recommend the reading to others and why or why not.

✧ Choose three of your classmates to ask you questions about your reading or to comment on your sharing.

# Rules for SSR Time

- ✧ Choose more to read than you think you will need.

- ✧ Have your materials ready before SSR time begins.

- ✧ If needed, get a drink and take a restroom break before SSR time begins.

- ✧ Find a comfortable place to read and stay there during SSR time.

- ✧ Keep your hands and feet to yourself. Stretch your arms out and be sure you cannot touch anyone else from where you are sitting in your reading place. If you can touch someone, move before you begin to read.

- ✧ Keep reading. Don't notice anything else while you are reading. The only exceptions are a fire drill, disaster drill, a call to the office, or instructions from your teacher.

- ✧ Stay quiet. Noise of any kind disturbs others and prevents you and them from reading.

# Integrated Strategies

# Oral Recitation Lesson

 **MATERIALS** ▸◆◆

◇ Reading selection for each student
◇ Story Map reproducible for each student (page 112)

**USE** ▸◆◆

◇ Whole Group
◇ Small Group
◇ Partner

**DESCRIPTION** ▸◆◆◆◆◆◆◆◆◆◆◆◆◆◆◆◆◆◆◆◆◆◆◆◆◆◆◆◆◆◆◆◆

The Oral Recitation Lesson is a structured process that involves both direct and indirect instruction using narrative text (Hoffman, 1987). The lesson includes the modeling of effective oral reading and both guided and independent practice. Reutzel and Hollingsworth (1993) and Reutzel, Hollingsworth, and Eldredge (1994) found that the Oral Recitation Lesson improves both fluency and reading comprehension.

**PROCEDURE** ▸◆◆

1. Read a story aloud to students.
2. Following the reading, elicit the major story elements, including setting, characters, major events, and solution. Individually or as a group, complete a story map graphic organizer. See page 112 for one example of a reproducible story map.
3. Using the story map as a guide, help students write a summary of the story. For students with little experience in summary writing, model how to write a summary using the information from the story map. For students who are more familiar with summary writing, you might use shared or interactive writing to complete the story summary. More advanced or more able students may be able to complete the summary independently.
4. Following the completion of the story map and summary, read aloud a selected portion of the story, perhaps one that was particularly exciting, meaningful, or eventful.

5. After reading the segment of the text aloud, have students read it chorally (see page 46) with you until they appear to be reading with good rate, accuracy, and expression.

6. Next, put students into pairs and have them read the story segment to each other. Ask students to read the passage just as you have practiced it together. Remind students that effective oral reading involves reading like they are talking, with accuracy and expression, for the purpose of communicating understanding.

7. When students have completed the partner reading, read aloud another portion of the text and follow it with Choral Reading (see page 46) and partner reading, until several segments of the text have been modeled and practiced.

8. On another day, ask students to select one of the modeled and practiced passages and read it aloud to a peer group. Following each reading, ask listeners to make one or two positive comments about each reader's performance.

9. On successive days (usually two to four), ask students to read aloud in a soft voice to themselves for about ten minutes, using the same passages previously practiced. Move around the class or group and listen to students as they read, providing feedback as appropriate.

## EVALUATION (student behaviors to look for)

✧ Quality of completed Story Map

✧ Active involvement in the group and partner readings

✧ Quality of soft voice reading (accuracy, speed, and expression) as you move about the room

# Story Map

Name _____ Date _____

**Title**

**Setting**

**Characters**

**Problem**

### Events

↓

↓

↓

**Solution/Outcome**

Based on Beck and McKeown (1981).
From Jerry L. Johns and Roberta L. Berglund, *Fluency: Strategies & Assessments* (3rd ed.). Copyright © 2006 Kendall/Hunt Publishing Company (1-800-247-3458, ext. 4 or 5). May be reproduced for noncommercial educational purposes.

# Book Bits

 **MATERIALS** ◆◆

✧ Reading selection

✧ Sentence or phrase strips for each student

✧ Book Bits reproducible for each student
(page 115)

 **USE** ◆◆

✧ Whole Group

**DESCRIPTION** ◆◆◆ ◆◆◆◆◆◆◆◆◆◆◆◆◆◆◆◆◆◆◆◆◆◆◆◆

Book Bits (Yopp & Yopp, 2003) combines fluency practice with the comprehension strategy of prediction. Students read short excerpts from a selection the class will be reading and then predict the content of the selection. Students also listen to other students read their excerpts and, as they do, they refine their predictions. Next, the selection is provided for the students to read. After reading, students may be asked to respond to the reading in one of a variety of ways (e.g., by completing a journal entry or posing questions for discussion).

**PROCEDURE** ◆◆

1. Select a text students will soon be reading.
2. Write short excerpts or sentences from the text on strips of paper. These excerpts are the Book Bits. Each student in the class or group should have a different excerpt.
3. Give each student a Book Bit.
4. Ask students to read their Book Bits silently.
5. Provide support to any student who appears to need help with the reading.

6. Ask students to write a brief prediction about the text. You could use the Book Bits reproducible master on page 115.

7. Have students move around the room, find a partner, and read their Book Bits to each other. Tell students that they must read exactly what is on their strip. They should not paraphrase or discuss it with their partners.

8. When partners have read their Book Bits to each other, each should find a different partner and repeat the procedure.

9. Continue this process until students have shared with several partners. You may want to tell students how many partners to share with. For example, "After you have shared your Book Bits with five classmates, return to your seats."

10. Have students return to their desks and write a new prediction based on the new information they have gathered.

11. Repeat steps 7–10.

12. Invite the group or class to share their predictions, how their predictions changed, or any questions they developed during the sharing.

13. Encourage some students to read their Book Bits aloud to support their predictions.

14. Have students read the text from which the Book Bits were taken.

15. After reading, invite students to respond to the selection with questions or connections they made as a result of the reading. You may choose to use the Book Bits reproducible master on page 115.

## EVALUATION (student behaviors to look for)

✧ Quality of responses on the Book Bits reproducible

✧ Quality of the expressive reading to partners

✧ Accuracy in reading the Book Bits

# Book Bits

Name _____ Date _____

Title _____

**Before Reading**

I think this will be about _____

_____

_____

_____

_____

Now I think _____

_____

_____

_____

I predict that _____

_____

_____

_____

_____

**After Reading**

This is what I think now _____

_____

_____

_____

Here are some questions I still have _____

_____

_____

_____

FLUENCY GOALS

COMPREHENSION · ACCURACY · SPEED · EXPRESSION

# Radio Reading

## ◆◆ MATERIALS ◆◆

✧ Reading selection
✧ Microphone or toy karaoke machine
(recommended for greater engagement)

## ◆◆ USE ◆◆

✧ Whole Group

## ◆◆◆ DESCRIPTION ◆◆◆ ◆◆◆◆◆◆◆◆◆◆◆◆◆◆◆◆◆◆◆◆◆◆◆◆

Radio Reading provides an opportunity for students to use their experiences with audio-only technology to model fluent reading and communicate a message to their peers (Greene, 1979; Searfoss, 1975). In Radio Reading, students read fluently for the purpose of performing and sharing a selected portion of text with others. Just as radio announcers do, they must read with expression at a comprehensible rate so that the listener can focus on the meaning and possible enjoyment of the passage. The procedure has four components: 1) getting started, 2) communicating the message, 3) checking for understanding, and 4) clarifying an unclear message (Searfoss, 1975). Opitz and Rasinski (1998) adapted the original procedure to allow students to practice preselected text prior to reading it aloud. For each portion of the text, one student assumes the role of the radio announcer, and the other students assume the roles of the radio listeners, just as they would when listening to an actual radio broadcast. Only the reader and the teacher have copies of the text open during the reading. All other students are active listeners with books closed. Allowing the reader to hold a microphone or use a toy karaoke machine should enhance the fun and increase motivation.

## ✖✦ PROCEDURE ▸✦✦

1. Select material that is at the student's instructional level. Materials at the student's instructional level are typically read with 95% accuracy.

2. On the day preceding the Radio Reading experience, explain the procedure to students. Emphasize that it is the reader's responsibility to communicate a message, much like a radio announcer does. Assign segments of text to students to prepare for the next day. These segments might be from a basal story the group has read, from a trade book or chapter book, from content area material, or from a student periodical.

3. Provide opportunities for students to practice their segments. This practice might be done with a buddy at school or with a parent or sibling at home.

4. In addition to practicing the selection, invite each student to prepare a question or two about the material that can be posed to the listeners following the reading. The questions might be literal or more open-ended, leading to discussion possibilities.

5. On the day you use Radio Reading, review with students the procedures listed below (and summarized on the following page) before beginning the session.

     ✧ The reader reads the assigned passage aloud with meaning and expression.

     ✧ If the reader miscalls a word, the reader is to correct it and go on reading, keeping the flow of the reading, and thus the meaning, intact.

     ✧ If the reader hesitates and can't quickly say a word, the reader may ask the teacher, "What is that word?" The teacher should immediately supply the word, thus preserving the message of the passage for listeners. If the reader hesitates and does not ask for help, the teacher waits a predetermined amount of time for the reader to supply the word (perhaps 5 seconds) and then tells the student the word.

     ✧ When the first student has finished reading, the questions he or she has prepared may be asked of the listeners right away or postponed until all of the reading has been completed. Listeners could also be asked to provide a quick summary of what they heard.

     ✧ If a reader has not communicated the message of the passage clearly or there is some confusion on the part of the listeners, then the reader is asked to reread the portion of text to help clarify and correct the confusion.

     ✧ Additional students then take turns reading their text segments for the listeners.

6. At the conclusion of the Radio Reading experience, each student then poses his or her questions to the group if they haven't already done so, or you may lead a brief discussion about the entire text. At this time, it may also be appropriate to reflect on the elements of effective read-alouds and how the group did in modeling them during the day's lesson.


## ✖✦ EVALUATION (student behaviors to look for) ▸✦✦

✧ Quality of questions and discussion

✧ Appropriate emphasis and expression

✧ Accuracy of word identification

✧ Quality of rereading to correct confusions

# Procedure for Radio Reading

1. Read your selection aloud with meaning and expression.

2. If you have trouble with a word:
   - ✧ correct it and go on.
   - ✧ ask, "What is that word?"

3. After reading:
   - ✧ ask the questions you have prepared for your selection.
   - ✧ ask someone to tell what your selection was mainly about.
   - ✧ reread portions of text to clarify and correct confusions.

# Part 3

## Passages and Resources for Fluency Checks

## Passages for Fluency Checks

# Overview

The graded passages for narrative and informational fluency checks range in difficulty from first through eighth grade. Passage difficulty was determined with the Fry (1968, 1977) and Spache (1953) readability formulas. The results of the readability checks and other information for the narrative passages are found in Table 5. Similar information for informational passages is found in Table 6.

The suggested procedure for using the graded passages for fluency checks is presented below.

1. Choose a graded passage at an appropriate level of difficulty. Give the Student Copy to the student and invite him or her to read it aloud for one minute. You will need a stopwatch or a watch with a second hand for timing. An alternate procedure is to time the student as the entire passage is read.

2. As the student reads, mark any miscues made on your Teacher Copy using a check mark (✓) or actually coding the nature of the miscues using the markings below or a system you typically use.

   **Miscues to Mark and Count as Errors**

   | | |
   |---|---|
   | Mispronunciation | scrape / scrap |
   | Substitution | men / man |
   | Omission | ~~men~~ |
   | Reversal | no / on |
   | Pause (3 seconds) | ᴾ reality (after 3 seconds, word is pronounced) |

   **Miscues Not Counted as Errors**

   | | |
   |---|---|
   | Insertion | little ∧ men |
   | Repetition | <u>men</u> |
   | Self-Correction | men sc / man |

3. At the end of one minute, ask the student to stop reading. Make a slash mark on your Teacher Copy after the last word the student read. Determine how many words were read in one minute by using the number at the end of the line and subtract any words not read. If the alternate procedure is used (reading the entire passage), note the time in seconds and place it as the divisor.

4. Ask one of the comprehension questions appropriate for the portion of the passage the student read. Alternate strategies include inviting a brief retelling or developing some questions of your own. The small

*Example*
Total Words
Read  _____

Errors
Counted  _____

WCPM  _____

circles with the numbers ❶ , ❷ , and ❸ indicate where the answer to the question is found in the passage.

5. On your Teacher Copy, note the total number of words read and subtract the errors from the total to arrive at words correct per minute (WCPM). See the example in the sidebar. Miscues that are generally counted as errors in this procedure include mispronunciations, substitutions, omissions, reversals, and pauses on words for at least three seconds. After three seconds, say the word for the student. Miscues that can be marked and not counted include repetitions, insertions, and self-corrections. An example of a student's reading is shown on page 123.

6. You may wish to reassess fluency with the same passage several times over the course of the school year. Note that the Teacher Copy contains provisions for a total of three readings. If you decide to have the student read the same passage again, use a different colored pen or pencil to note miscues and the total number of words read.

7. Student results can be kept in individual portfolios or folders. The results can also be used as a Classroom Fluency Snapshot (see pages 11–14) by placing them on one of the Class Fluency Records on pages 158–159. You may also want to use the Fluency Rubric on page 161.

8. To note the student's progress in fluency within a grade and for subsequent grades, use the Cumulative Record for Fluency Checks on page 162.

**TABLE 5**  Readability Ratings for the Narrative Passages

| GRADE | PASSAGE | TITLE | NUMBER OF WORDS | FRY READABILITY | SPACHE READABILITY |
|-------|---------|-------|-----------------|-----------------|--------------------|
| 1 | N 7141 | Blue | 151 | 1 | 1.5 |
| 2 | N 8224 | My Birthday | 160 | 2 | 1.9 |
| 3 | N 3183 | Elephant Farm | 171 | 3 | 2.4 |
| 4 | N 5414 | Living in China | 184 | 4 | — |
| 5 | N 8595 | Paper Route | 191 | 5 | — |
| 6 | N 6867 | Impressions of America | 199 | 6 | — |
| 7 | N 3717 | Imagination | 213 | 7 | — |
| 8 | N 8183 | Inventions | 219 | 8 | — |

**TABLE 6**  Readability Ratings for Informational Passages

| GRADE | PASSAGE | TITLE | NUMBER OF WORDS | FRY READABILITY | SPACHE READABILITY |
|---|---|---|---|---|---|
| 1 | I 7141 | Tadpoles | 107 | 1 | 1.8 |
| 2 | I 8224 | Weather | 119 | 2 | 2.0 |
| 3 | I 3183 | The Earth's Hemispheres | 135 | 3 | 2.3 |
| 4 | I 5414 | Milk | 146 | 4 | — |
| 5 | I 8595 | The Uncommon, Common Pet | 163 | 5 | — |
| 6 | I 6867 | Nashville's Music | 172 | 6 | — |
| 7 | I 3717 | Ronald Reagan, An American Hero | 189 | 7 | — |
| 8 | I 8183 | Ballet | 204 | 8 | — |

# Example of Student's Reading

N 3183 (Grade 3)

### Elephant Farm

Every year the third grade goes into the mountains to visit
an elephant farm. Today our class finally went.

As we walked to the farm, <u>we bought bananas</u> from women
*brought sc*  ❶
along the path. Monkeys were hanging in the trees chattering
*are\**
for a banana. Monkeys are cute, but I came to see elephants!
*\*   s*

I was looking for an elephant, when I felt someone standing
behind me. I turned around. A huge gray shape was there! I
could not see the top! I stepped back and saw the elephant's
❷
kind eye. I <u>held</u> up a banana. He took it in his trunk and put it
*← end of 1 minute*
in his/mouth. He ate the whole thing, peel and all!

Soon it was my turn to ride an elephant. Riding an elephant
❸
feels like rocking in a boat in choppy water. I was holding on
for my life! My friend told me to relax and sit like a wet
noodle. Then I could roll with the elephant's walk. I will never
forget my first day with elephants.

*counted as error (see p. 80)

$$)\overline{10{,}260}$$

__+__ ❶ What did they buy on the way to the
farm? (<u>bananas</u>)

_____ ❷ What was standing behind the author?
(an elephant)

_____ ❸ What does it feel like to ride an
elephant? (like rocking in a boat in
choppy water)

### Reading and Miscues Counted as Errors

| | 1st | 2nd | 3rd |
|---|---|---|---|
| 11 | ____ | ____ | ____ |
| 19 | ____ | ____ | ____ |
| 30 | ____ | ____ | ____ |
| 40 | / | ____ | ____ |
| 52 | / | ____ | ____ |
| 63 | ____ | ____ | ____ |
| 75 | ____ | ____ | ____ |
| 87 | ____ | ____ | ____ |
| 103 | ____ | ____ | ____ |
| 114 | ____ | ____ | ____ |
| 126 | ____ | ____ | ____ |
| 139 | ____ | ____ | ____ |
| 153 | ____ | ____ | ____ |
| 165 | ____ | ____ | ____ |
| 171 | ____ | ____ | ____ |

| | 1st | 2nd | 3rd |
|---|---|---|---|
| Total Words Read | 105 | ____ | ____ |
| Errors Counted | − 2 | − | − |
| WCPM | 103 | | |

| Norm Group Percentile from Table 2, page 6 | 1st | 2nd | 3rd |
|---|---|---|---|
| | ☐ 90 | ☐ 90 | ☐ 90 |
| | ☐ 75 | ☐ 75 | ☐ 75 |
| | ☑ 50+ | ☐ 50 | ☐ 50 |
| | ☐ 25 | ☐ 25 | ☐ 25 |
| | ☐ 10 | ☐ 10 | ☐ 10 |
| Date | Winter 2/8/06 | ____ | ____ |

| | Seldom Weak Poor | | Always Strong Excellent |
|---|---|---|---|
| Phrasing | ├————┼————X——┤ |
| Expression | ├————┼———X———┤ |
| Punctuation | ├————┼————X┤ |
| Rate | ├————┼—X————┤ |

## Blue

One day Joe looked for his dog, Blue. He wanted to play ball. But Joe could not find Blue. Joe looked in his room. He looked in the kitchen. He looked under the table. He looked on the couch. He looked all around the house. Blue could not be found anywhere.

Joe went outside. He was sitting by a tree when he heard something. He turned his head. He heard it again. Joe walked toward the old well. There had not been any water in it for a long time. He looked into the well and saw a small black and white face looking up at him. It was Blue! He called to his father. His father knew how to get Blue out.

Blue was happy to get out of the well. He ran in circles around Joe. Joe laughed. Hide and seek was a new game to play with Blue.

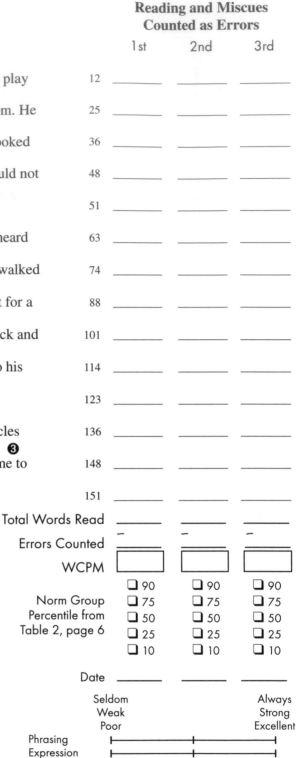

Blue ❶

One day Joe looked for his dog, Blue. He wanted to play

ball. But Joe could not find Blue. Joe looked in his room. He

looked in the kitchen. He looked under the table. He looked

on the couch. He looked all around the house. Blue could not

be found anywhere.

Joe went outside. He was sitting by a tree when he heard

something. He turned his head. He heard it again. Joe walked

toward the old well. There had not been any water in it for a

long time. He looked into the well and saw a small black and

white face looking up at him. It was Blue! He called to his

father. His father knew how to get Blue out. ❷

Blue was happy to get out of the well. He ran in circles

around Joe. Joe laughed. Hide and seek was a new game to ❸

play with Blue.

| | 1st | 2nd | 3rd |
|---|---|---|---|
| 12 | | | |
| 25 | | | |
| 36 | | | |
| 48 | | | |
| 51 | | | |
| 63 | | | |
| 74 | | | |
| 88 | | | |
| 101 | | | |
| 114 | | | |
| 123 | | | |
| 136 | | | |
| 148 | | | |
| 151 | | | |
| Total Words Read | | | |
| Errors Counted | | | |
| WCPM | | | |

)9060

_____ ❶ What was Joe looking for? (his dog; Blue)

_____ ❷ How did Blue get out of the well? (Joe's father got him)

_____ ❸ What new game had Blue played with Joe? (hide and seek)

| Norm Group Percentile from Table 2, page 6 | ❑ 90 ❑ 75 ❑ 50 ❑ 25 ❑ 10 | ❑ 90 ❑ 75 ❑ 50 ❑ 25 ❑ 10 | ❑ 90 ❑ 75 ❑ 50 ❑ 25 ❑ 10 |
|---|---|---|---|

Date _____ _____ _____

| | Seldom Weak Poor | | Always Strong Excellent |
|---|---|---|---|
| Phrasing | ⊢————⊢————⊣ | | |
| Expression | ⊢————⊢————⊣ | | |
| Punctuation | ⊢————⊢————⊣ | | |
| Rate | ⊢————⊢————⊣ | | |

## My Birthday

I turn seven in two weeks. I have lots of ideas to make it the best birthday I ever had. First, I want my four best friends to spend the day with me. A big, black train will take us to a farm. The conductor will let me blow the whistle seven times. At the farm, we will see cows, ducks, chickens, and horses. Then we will have a picnic lunch with ice cream and cake. After lunch, we will ride in a hot air balloon. We will fly high in the sky! We will fly over my school! After the balloon ride, I hope to find a new bicycle in the back of our truck. If I don't get a bicycle, maybe a new puppy will be waiting for me at home. After dark we will catch fireflies. We will put them in jars to make firefly lanterns. Can you imagine a better way to spend your seventh birthday?

## My Birthday

| | | 1st | 2nd | 3rd |
|---|---|---|---|---|
| I turn seven in two weeks. I have lots of ideas to make it the | 15 | _____ | _____ | _____ |
| ❶ best birthday I ever had. First, I want my four best friends to | 28 | _____ | _____ | _____ |
| spend the day with me. A big, black train will take us to a farm. ❷ | 43 | _____ | _____ | _____ |
| The conductor will let me blow the whistle seven times. At the | 55 | _____ | _____ | _____ |
| farm, we will see cows, ducks, chickens, and horses. Then we | 66 | _____ | _____ | _____ |
| will have a picnic lunch with ice cream and cake. After lunch, | 78 | _____ | _____ | _____ |
| ❸ we will ride in a hot air balloon. We will fly high in the sky! | 93 | _____ | _____ | _____ |
| We will fly over my school! After the balloon ride, I hope to | 106 | _____ | _____ | _____ |
| find a new bicycle in the back of our truck. If I don't get a | 121 | _____ | _____ | _____ |
| bicycle, maybe a new puppy will be waiting for me at home. | 133 | _____ | _____ | _____ |
| After dark we will catch fireflies. We will put them in jars to | 146 | _____ | _____ | _____ |
| make firefly lanterns. Can you imagine a better way to spend | 157 | _____ | _____ | _____ |
| your seventh birthday? | 160 | _____ | _____ | _____ |

$$9600$$

| | 1st | 2nd | 3rd |
|---|---|---|---|
| Total Words Read | _____ | _____ | _____ |
| Errors Counted | ‒ | ‒ | ‒ |
| WCPM | ☐ | ☐ | ☐ |

_____ ❶ What is being celebrated? (a birthday)

_____ ❷ Where will they go? (to a farm)

_____ ❸ What will they do there? (see animals; have a picnic lunch; take a ride in a hot air balloon [any 2])

| Norm Group Percentile from Table 2, page 6 | | |
|---|---|---|
| ❏ 90 | ❏ 90 | ❏ 90 |
| ❏ 75 | ❏ 75 | ❏ 75 |
| ❏ 50 | ❏ 50 | ❏ 50 |
| ❏ 25 | ❏ 25 | ❏ 25 |
| ❏ 10 | ❏ 10 | ❏ 10 |

Date _____ _____ _____

| | Seldom Weak Poor | | Always Strong Excellent |
|---|---|---|---|
| Phrasing | ├──────────┼──────────┤ |
| Expression | ├──────────┼──────────┤ |
| Punctuation | ├──────────┼──────────┤ |
| Rate | ├──────────┼──────────┤ |

## Elephant Farm

Every year the third grade goes into the mountains to visit an elephant farm. Today our class finally went.

As we walked to the farm, we bought bananas from women along the path. Monkeys were hanging in the trees chattering for a banana. Monkeys are cute, but I came to see elephants!

I was looking for an elephant when I felt someone standing behind me. I turned around. A huge gray shape was there! I could not see the top! I stepped back and saw the elephant's kind eye. I held up a banana. He took it in his trunk and put it in his mouth. He ate the whole thing, peel and all!

Soon it was my turn to ride an elephant. Riding an elephant feels like rocking in a boat in choppy water. I was holding on for my life! My friend told me to relax and sit like a wet noodle. Then I could roll with the elephant's walk. I will never forget my first day with elephants.

### Elephant Farm

| | **Reading and Miscues Counted as Errors** | | |
|---|---|---|---|
| | 1st | 2nd | 3rd |

Every year the third grade goes into the mountains to visit 11 _____ _____ _____

an elephant farm. Today our class finally went. ❶ 19 _____ _____ _____

As we walked to the farm, we bought bananas from women 30 _____ _____ _____

along the path. Monkeys were hanging in the trees chattering 40 _____ _____ _____

for a banana. Monkeys are cute, but I came to see elephants! 52 _____ _____ _____

I was looking for an elephant when I felt someone standing 63 _____ _____ _____

behind me. I turned around. A huge gray shape was there! I 75 _____ _____ _____

could not see the top! I stepped back and saw the elephant's 87 _____ _____ _____

❷ kind eye. I held up a banana. He took it in his trunk and put it 103 _____ _____ _____

in his mouth. He ate the whole thing, peel and all! 114 _____ _____ _____

Soon it was my turn to ride an elephant. Riding an elephant 126 _____ _____ _____

❸ feels like rocking in a boat in choppy water. I was holding on 139 _____ _____ _____

for my life! My friend told me to relax and sit like a wet 153 _____ _____ _____

noodle. Then I could roll with the elephant's walk. I will never 165 _____ _____ _____

forget my first day with elephants. 171 _____ _____ _____

$$\overline{)10,260}$$

| | 1st | 2nd | 3rd |
|---|---|---|---|
| Total Words Read | _____ | _____ | _____ |
| Errors Counted | ‾ | ‾ | ‾ |
| WCPM | [ ] | [ ] | [ ] |

| Norm Group Percentile from Table 2, page 6 | ❑ 90 | ❑ 90 | ❑ 90 |
|---|---|---|---|
| | ❑ 75 | ❑ 75 | ❑ 75 |
| | ❑ 50 | ❑ 50 | ❑ 50 |
| | ❑ 25 | ❑ 25 | ❑ 25 |
| | ❑ 10 | ❑ 10 | ❑ 10 |

Date _____ _____ _____

| | Seldom Weak Poor | | Always Strong Excellent |
|---|---|---|---|
| Phrasing | ├───────┼───────┤ |
| Expression | ├───────┼───────┤ |
| Punctuation | ├───────┼───────┤ |
| Rate | ├───────┼───────┤ |

_____ ❶ What did they buy on the way to the farm? (bananas)

_____ ❷ What was standing behind the author? (an elephant)

_____ ❸ What does it feel like to ride an elephant? (like rocking in a boat in choppy water)

### Living in China

Last year, my family moved to China when my dad got a promotion. I thought it would be terrible to live in another country, leaving my friends and school behind.

After we got here, I realized China would be the ultimate adventure. Every day I look for something new. This morning I cut through the market to catch the bus. Halfway down the fruit row, a vendor offered me some green fruit. As I looked at the unripe ball, she peeled it for me. Just to be polite, I took a bite. A familiar sweet juice exploded in my mouth. It was a green orange!

I spend a lot of time on the bus going to school. It's a great place to learn about China. I practice my Chinese by listening to people conversing around me. People are friendly and look out for me. The bus is crowded, and sometimes I have trouble getting to the door. Once some passengers helped me climb out a window at my stop.

Although I was unenthusiastic about moving at first, now I'm impatient for tomorrow's new adventures.

## Reading and Miscues Counted as Errors

| | 1st | 2nd | 3rd |
|---|---|---|---|

### Living in China

Last year, my family moved to China when my dad got a ❶ 12 ____ ____ ____

promotion. I thought it would be terrible to live in another 23 ____ ____ ____

country, leaving my friends and school behind. 30 ____ ____ ____

After we got here, I realized China would be the ultimate 41 ____ ____ ____

adventure. Every day I look for something new. This morning I 52 ____ ____ ____

cut through the market to catch the bus. Halfway down the fruit 64 ____ ____ ____

row, a vendor offered me some green fruit. As I looked at the 77 ____ ____ ____

unripe ball, she peeled it for me. Just to be polite, I took a bite. 92 ____ ____ ____

A familiar sweet juice exploded in my mouth. It was a green 104 ____ ____ ____

orange! ❷ 105 ____ ____ ____

I spend a lot of time on the bus going to school. It's a great 120 ____ ____ ____

place to learn about China. I practice my Chinese by listening 131 ____ ____ ____

to people conversing around me. People are friendly and look 141 ____ ____ ____

out for me. The bus is crowded, and sometimes I have trouble 153 ____ ____ ____

getting to the door. Once some passengers helped me climb out 164 ____ ____ ____

a window at my stop. ❸ 169 ____ ____ ____

Although I was unenthusiastic about moving at first, now 178 ____ ____ ____

I'm impatient for tomorrow's new adventures. 184 ____ ____ ____

$\overline{)11,040}$

| | | | |
|---|---|---|---|
| Total Words Read | ____ | ____ | ____ |
| Errors Counted | – | – | – |
| WCPM | [ ] | [ ] | [ ] |

| | 1st | 2nd | 3rd |
|---|---|---|---|
| Norm Group Percentile from Table 2, page 6 | ❏ 90 ❏ 75 ❏ 50 ❏ 25 ❏ 10 | ❏ 90 ❏ 75 ❏ 50 ❏ 25 ❏ 10 | ❏ 90 ❏ 75 ❏ 50 ❏ 25 ❏ 10 |
| Date | ____ | ____ | ____ |

____ ❶ How did the author feel about moving to China? (terrible)

____ ❷ What surprise did the author find at the market? (a green orange)

____ ❸ What happened when the author couldn't get to the bus door? (passengers helped him or her climb out the window)

| | Seldom Weak Poor | | Always Strong Excellent |
|---|---|---|---|
| Phrasing | ├──────── | ──────┼───── | ──────┤ |
| Expression | ├──────── | ──────┼───── | ──────┤ |
| Punctuation | ├──────── | ──────┼───── | ──────┤ |
| Rate | ├──────── | ──────┼───── | ──────┤ |

Paper Route

I've had a newspaper route since I was nine years old. Every afternoon the papers are delivered to my house in a bundle. Right after school I count and fold the newspapers. This is messy work, since the ink transfers onto my hands.

Usually I walk my newspaper route, but sometimes I wear my roller blades. I need to hurry to deliver the papers before supper, but I can't be careless. Each customer has a preferred place for the paper to be left. I try not to walk on the grass, since it might damage someone's lawn.

Generally my customers are good-natured. Many give me a bonus or a present for Christmas. Once someone gave me a whole pound of chocolates!

My favorite customers are a retired couple who invite me inside every day. In the winter they give me hot cocoa to warm me from the inside out. In the summer, they always have ice cold lemonade. We talk about everything from our favorite books to the best kind of ice cream. They are my adopted grandparents.

Maybe next summer I will have saved enough money to buy a bicycle.

**Reading and Miscues
Counted as Errors**

| | 1st | 2nd | 3rd |
|---|---|---|---|

### Paper Route

I've had a newspaper route since I was nine years old.   11

Every afternoon the papers are delivered to my house in a   22

bundle. Right after school I count and fold the newspapers. ❶   32

This is messy work, since the ink transfers onto my hands.   43

Usually I walk my newspaper route, but sometimes I wear   53

my roller blades. I need to hurry to deliver the papers before   65

supper, ❷ but I can't be careless. Each customer has a preferred   76

place for the paper to be left. I try not to walk on the grass,   91

since it might damage someone's lawn.   97

Generally my customers are good-natured. Many give me   105

a bonus or a present for Christmas. Once someone gave me a   117

whole pound of chocolates!   121

My favorite customers are a retired couple who invite me   131

inside every day. In the winter they give me hot cocoa to warm   144

❸ me from the inside out. In the summer, they always have ice   156

cold lemonade. We talk about everything from our favorite   165

books to the best kind of ice cream. They are my adopted   177

grandparents.   178

Maybe next summer I will have saved enough money to   188

buy a bicycle.   191

$\overline{)11,460}$

____ ❶ What is the first thing the newspaper carrier must do after school? (count and fold the newspapers)

____ ❷ When must the newspapers be delivered by? (before supper)

____ ❸ Who are the newspaper carrier's favorite customers? (a retired couple who invites him or her in for something to drink)

| | 1st | 2nd | 3rd |
|---|---|---|---|
| Total Words Read | | | |
| Errors Counted | | | |
| WCPM | | | |

| Norm Group Percentile from Table 2, page 6 | 1st | 2nd | 3rd |
|---|---|---|---|
| | ❏ 90 | ❏ 90 | ❏ 90 |
| | ❏ 75 | ❏ 75 | ❏ 75 |
| | ❏ 50 | ❏ 50 | ❏ 50 |
| | ❏ 25 | ❏ 25 | ❏ 25 |
| | ❏ 10 | ❏ 10 | ❏ 10 |

Date _____  _____  _____

| | Seldom Weak Poor | | Always Strong Excellent |
|---|---|---|---|
| Phrasing | ├────────┼────────┤ | | |
| Expression | ├────────┼────────┤ | | |
| Punctuation | ├────────┼────────┤ | | |
| Rate | ├────────┼────────┤ | | |

Impressions of America

I am a sixth grade Japanese exchange student in Illinois. I live with my American parents in a tiny, rural town. There are a lot of farms where soybeans are grown.

At first, I was scared to go to American school, even though my American sister is also in sixth grade. Soon I realized there was nothing to fear. Most Americans are friendly. They talk openly and directly the first time they meet me. In Japan, I might not talk to my classmates the whole semester!

My hometown is a crowded suburb of Tokyo. The wide-open prairie in Illinois is very different. There are no buildings blocking my view of the sky. American houses keep each other at arm's length, not like a cozy Japanese neighborhood where houses playfully bump elbows.

I may never adjust to American houses, but it's easy to adjust to American cars. I love to jump in the car to go anywhere. It might be possible to do everything in America without getting out of the car. I can buy food, visit the bank, fill prescriptions and see a movie.

It will be fun to tell my family about American life. Won't they be amazed?

**Reading and Miscues
Counted as Errors**

|  | 1st | 2nd | 3rd |
|---|---|---|---|

Impressions of America ❶

I am a sixth grade Japanese exchange student in Illinois. I    11

live with my American parents in a tiny, rural town. There are a    24

lot of farms where soybeans are grown.    31

At first, I was scared to go to American school, even though    43

my American sister is also in sixth grade. Soon I realized there    55

was nothing to fear. Most Americans are friendly. They talk    65

openly and directly the first time they meet me. In Japan, I    77

might not talk to my classmates the whole semester!    86

My hometown is a crowded suburb of Tokyo. The wide-    96

open prairie in Illinois is very different. There are no buildings    106

blocking my view of the sky. American houses keep each other    117

at arm's length, not like a cozy Japanese neighborhood where    127

houses playfully bump elbows. ❷    131

I may never adjust to American houses, but it's easy to    142

adjust to American cars. I love to jump in the car to go    155

anywhere. It might be possible to do everything in America    165

without getting out of the car. I can buy food, visit the bank,    178

fill prescriptions and see a movie.    184

It will be fun to tell my family about American life. Won't    196

they be amazed?    199

)11,940

Total Words Read _____ _____ _____

Errors Counted _____ _____ _____

WCPM

| | 1st | 2nd | 3rd |
|---|---|---|---|
| Norm Group | ☐ 90 | ☐ 90 | ☐ 90 |
| Percentile from | ☐ 75 | ☐ 75 | ☐ 75 |
| Table 2, page 6 | ☐ 50 | ☐ 50 | ☐ 50 |
| | ☐ 25 | ☐ 25 | ☐ 25 |
| | ☐ 10 | ☐ 10 | ☐ 10 |

_____ ❶ Where was the exchange student
          from? (Japan)

_____ ❷ How do Japanese and American
          homes differ? (Japanese homes are
          built close together; American homes
          are spread far apart)

_____ ❸ What does the student enjoy about
          American cars? (being able to do
          everything without getting out of the
          car)

Date _____ _____ _____

|  | Seldom / Weak / Poor |  | Always / Strong / Excellent |
|---|---|---|---|
| Phrasing | ├───────┼───────┤ |
| Expression | ├───────┼───────┤ |
| Punctuation | ├───────┼───────┤ |
| Rate | ├───────┼───────┤ |

From Jerry L. Johns and Roberta L. Berglund, *Fluency: Strategies & Assessments* (3rd ed.). Copyright © 2006 Kendall/Hunt Publishing Company (1-800-247-3458, ext. 4 or 5). May be reproduced for noncommercial educational purposes.

Imagination

Do you use your imagination enough? Too much of youth is spent doing chores, eating healthy food, and going to school. There's no room for the imagination in these mundane trivialities. In my imagination, I can outwit the biggest bully, mysteriously save the world, and effortlessly keep my room clean.

I need to imagine a way to persuade my teachers and parents to see the benefits of my imagination. Unhindered, I could suggest solutions to all kinds of everyday problems. Imagine if there were a self-cleaning fabric for clothes. Humanity would forever be liberated from laundry! Adults think I have an extensive imagination already, which needs no further development.

I should write my ideas in a journal. Everyone could reap the rewards of my great imagination. I hope it never falls into the wrong hands. What if someone put it up for ransom? Maybe I can imagine a place where no one will find it. Hopefully my imagination won't get away from me so that I forget where I hide it. All of that knowledge would be lost. Maybe a kid will find it in a hundred years and profit from my exceptional ideas. Then my imagination would be a success! Now I need to imagine a way to pay for my journal.

## Reading and Miscues Counted as Errors

| | 1st | 2nd | 3rd |
|---|---|---|---|

### Imagination

Do you use your imagination enough? Too much of youth is 11
spent doing chores, eating healthy food, and going to school. 21
There's no room for the imagination in these mundane 30
trivialities. In my imagination, I can outwit the biggest bully, 40
mysteriously save the world, and effortlessly keep my room 49
clean. ❶ 50

I need to imagine a way to persuade my teachers and 61
parents to see the benefits of my imagination. Unhindered, I 71
could suggest solutions to all kinds of everyday problems. 80
Imagine if there were a self-cleaning fabric for clothes. 89
Humanity would forever be liberated from laundry! Adults 97
think I have an extensive imagination already, which needs no 107
further development. ❷ 109

I should write my ideas in a journal. Everyone could reap 120
the rewards of my great imagination. I hope it never falls into 132
the wrong hands. What if someone put it up for ransom? 143
Maybe I can imagine a place where no one will find it. 155
Hopefully my imagination won't get away from me so that I 166
forget where I hide it. ❸ All of that knowledge would be lost. 178
Maybe a kid will find it in a hundred years and profit from my 192
exceptional ideas. Then my imagination would be a success! 201
Now I need to imagine a way to pay for my journal. 213

$$\overline{)12{,}780}$$

Total Words Read ____

Errors Counted ‾  ‾  ‾

WCPM [ ] [ ] [ ]

| Norm Group Percentile from Table 2, page 6 | ❏ 90 ❏ 75 ❏ 50 ❏ 25 ❏ 10 | ❏ 90 ❏ 75 ❏ 50 ❏ 25 ❏ 10 | ❏ 90 ❏ 75 ❏ 50 ❏ 25 ❏ 10 |
|---|---|---|---|

Date ____  ____  ____

| | Seldom Weak Poor | | Always Strong Excellent |
|---|---|---|---|
| Phrasing | ├───────┼───────┤ | | |
| Expression | ├───────┼───────┤ | | |
| Punctuation | ├───────┼───────┤ | | |
| Rate | ├───────┼───────┤ | | |

____ ❶ What has the author imagined being able to do? (outwit the biggest bully; save the world; keep his or her room clean without effort [any 2])

____ ❷ Where does the author plan to record his or her ideas? (in a journal)

____ ❸ What does the author fear? (losing his or her journal; forgetting where it was put)

Inventions

Has everything been invented? Is there a book that lists
what still needs to be invented? Ordinary things like umbrellas,
telescopes, zippers, typewriters, guitars, and tools to fix things
are already invented. I want to be a pioneer and create
something new like Thomas Edison. I read a book about him
and learned that he invented many things besides the light bulb.
He patented over 1,000 inventions. He was probably the
greatest inventor in American history.

Inventions solve problems, make life more comfortable,
orbit in the sky thousands of miles away, and satisfy curiosities.
Then they get put in museums when another invention is
created that is smaller and faster. Perhaps yesterday's
inventions should get recycled into art and be displayed in an
art museum.

Inventing is a mystery to me. I am quite surprised by the
suffering some inventors go through to perfect their creations.
They cannot be careless. Yet they must take risks while being
cautious and steady. What motivates their great sacrifices?
Maybe the thrill of perfecting their creation precisely as they
dreamed is deeply satisfying.

I plan to go to a museum to marvel at some old inventions.
I hope to be inspired to design something yet to be invented.
One day my name might be as recognizable as the great
American inventor Thomas Edison.

**Reading and Miscues Counted as Errors**

| | 1st | 2nd | 3rd |
|---|---|---|---|

### Inventions

Has everything been invented? Is there a book that lists what still needs to be invented? Ordinary things like umbrellas, telescopes, zippers, typewriters, guitars, and tools to fix things are already invented. I want to be a pioneer and create something new like Thomas Edison. I read a book about him and learned that he invented many things besides the light bulb. He patented over 1,000 inventions. He was probably the greatest inventor in American history.

Inventions solve problems, make life more comfortable, orbit in the sky thousands of miles away, and satisfy curiosities. Then they get put in museums when another invention is created that is smaller and faster. Perhaps yesterday's inventions should get recycled into art and be displayed in an art museum.

Inventing is a mystery to me. I am quite surprised by the suffering some inventors go through to perfect their creations. They cannot be careless. Yet they must take risks while being cautious and steady. What motivates their great sacrifices? Maybe the thrill of perfecting their creation precisely as they dreamed is deeply satisfying.

I plan to go to a museum to marvel at some old inventions. I hope to be inspired to design something yet to be invented. One day my name might be as recognizable as the great American inventor Thomas Edison.

| Line | 1st | 2nd | 3rd |
|---|---|---|---|
| 10 | | | |
| 20 | | | |
| 29 | | | |
| 40 | | | |
| 51 | | | |
| 62 | | | |
| 71 | | | |
| 76 | | | |
| 83 | | | |
| 94 | | | |
| 104 | | | |
| 112 | | | |
| 123 | | | |
| 125 | | | |
| 137 | | | |
| 146 | | | |
| 157 | | | |
| 165 | | | |
| 175 | | | |
| 179 | | | |
| 192 | | | |
| 204 | | | |
| 215 | | | |
| 219 | | | |

Total Words Read ____  ____  ____

Errors Counted ____  ____  ____

WCPM ☐  ☐  ☐

$\overline{)13{,}140}$

____  ❶ What does the author wonder? (if everything has been invented; if there is a book listing what still needs to be invented)

____  ❷ What does the author believe should happen to old inventions? (they should get recycled into art and go on display in an art museum)

____  ❸ How does the author describe inventors? (suffering; risk-takers; cautious; steady; perfectionists [any 2])

Norm Group Percentile from Table 2, page 6

| | 1st | 2nd | 3rd |
|---|---|---|---|
| | ☐ 90 | ☐ 90 | ☐ 90 |
| | ☐ 75 | ☐ 75 | ☐ 75 |
| | ☐ 50 | ☐ 50 | ☐ 50 |
| | ☐ 25 | ☐ 25 | ☐ 25 |
| | ☐ 10 | ☐ 10 | ☐ 10 |

Date ____  ____  ____

| | Seldom Weak Poor | | Always Strong Excellent |
|---|---|---|---|
| Phrasing | ├——————┼——————┤ |
| Expression | ├——————┼——————┤ |
| Punctuation | ├——————┼——————┤ |
| Rate | ├——————┼——————┤ |

From Jerry L. Johns and Roberta L. Berglund, *Fluency: Strategies & Assessments* (3rd ed.). Copyright © 2006 Kendall/Hunt Publishing Company (1-800-247-3458, ext. 4 or 5). May be reproduced for noncommercial educational purposes.

## Tadpoles

Tadpoles are baby frogs. They live in water. They look and act like fish. When they are born, tadpoles have no legs. They only have a tail. The tail helps them swim. Tadpoles eat water plants and seaweed. They will swim to the bottom of the pond to eat dead animals.

Tadpoles spend winter sleeping in mud. They begin to grow legs in summer. It takes them a year to become frogs. As they grow legs, they swim less. The tail becomes part of the body. They spend more time at the top of the pond. They begin to breathe air. Soon the tadpole is a frog.

## Tadpoles

**❶**

Tadpoles are baby frogs. They live in water. They look and    11 ___ ___ ___

act like fish. When they are born, tadpoles have no legs. They    23 ___ ___ ___

**❷**

only have a tail. The tail helps them swim. Tadpoles eat water    35 ___ ___ ___

plants and seaweed. They will swim to the bottom of the pond to    48 ___ ___ ___

eat dead animals.    51 ___ ___ ___

Tadpoles spend winter sleeping in mud. They begin to grow    61 ___ ___ ___

legs in summer. It takes them a year to become frogs. As they    74 ___ ___ ___

**❸**

grow legs, they swim less. The tail becomes part of the body.    86 ___ ___ ___

They spend more time at the top of the pond. They begin to    99 ___ ___ ___

breathe air. Soon the tadpole is a frog.    107 ___ ___ ___

$$\overline{)6{,}420}$$

| | | |
|---|---|---|
| Total Words Read | ___ ___ ___ |
| Errors Counted | – – – |
| WCPM | [ ] [ ] [ ] |

_____ ❶ What are "tadpoles"? (baby frogs)

Norm Group
Percentile from
Table 2, page 6

❏ 90 ❏ 90 ❏ 90
❏ 75 ❏ 75 ❏ 75
❏ 50 ❏ 50 ❏ 50
❏ 25 ❏ 25 ❏ 25
❏ 10 ❏ 10 ❏ 10

_____ ❷ What do tadpoles look like? (like fish; no legs; only a tail)

Date ___ ___ ___

_____ ❸ How do tadpoles change as they grow into frogs? (they grow legs, the tail becomes part of the body)

| | Seldom<br>Weak<br>Poor | | Always<br>Strong<br>Excellent |
|---|---|---|---|
| Phrasing | ⊢ | ⊣ | ⊣ |
| Expression | ⊢ | ⊣ | ⊣ |
| Punctuation | ⊢ | ⊣ | ⊣ |
| Rate | ⊢ | ⊣ | ⊣ |

## Weather

Weather is a word that tells people what it is like outside. The weather might be rainy. The weather might be cold. The weather might be clear. Some people study the weather. They measure the temperature. They measure how fast the wind blows. They measure how much snow and rain fall.

People use this information to make plans. Farmers know when to plant their crops. Sports teams plan when to play. Parents know what their children should wear to school. Children may decide whether they should play inside or outside. If bad weather is coming, people can make plans to be safe. There are many good reasons to know about weather. What kind of weather do you like best?

Weather

| | 1st | 2nd | 3rd |
|---|---|---|---|

Weather is a word that tells people what it is like outside. 12

The weather might be rainy. The weather might be cold. The 23

❶

weather might be clear. Some people study the weather. They 33

measure the temperature. They measure how fast the wind blows. 43

They measure how much snow and rain fall. ❷ 51

People use this information to make plans. Farmers know 60

when to plant their crops. Sports teams plan when to play. Parents 72

know what their children should wear to school. Children may 82

decide whether they should play inside or outside. If bad weather 93

❸

is coming, people can make plans to be safe. There are many 105

good reasons to know about weather. What kind of weather do 116

you like best? 119

$$\overline{)7140}$$

| | | | |
|---|---|---|---|
| Total Words Read | | | |
| Errors Counted | | | |
| WCPM | | | |

_____ ❶ What is one kind of weather? (rainy; cold; clear)

_____ ❷ What is a part of weather people can measure? (temperature; wind speed; snow fall; rain fall [any 2])

_____ ❸ Why do people study weather? (so they can make plans for the future; plan what to grow; plan when to play; plan what to wear; plan where to play; plan for safety [any 2])

| Norm Group Percentile from Table 2, page 6 | ❏ 90 ❏ 75 ❏ 50 ❏ 25 ❏ 10 | ❏ 90 ❏ 75 ❏ 50 ❏ 25 ❏ 10 | ❏ 90 ❏ 75 ❏ 50 ❏ 25 ❏ 10 |
|---|---|---|---|

Date _____  _____  _____

| | Seldom Weak Poor | | Always Strong Excellent |
|---|---|---|---|
| Phrasing | ⊢ | ┼ | ⊣ |
| Expression | ⊢ | ┼ | ⊣ |
| Punctuation | ⊢ | ┼ | ⊣ |
| Rate | ⊢ | ┼ | ⊣ |

Adapted from O'Hare, T. (2003). *Studying weather: Weather report.* Vero Beach, FL: Rourke Publishing. From Jerry L. Johns and Roberta L. Berglund, *Fluency: Strategies & Assessments* (3rd ed.). Copyright © 2006 Kendall/Hunt Publishing Company (1-800-247-3458, ext. 4 or 5). May be reproduced for noncommercial educational purposes.

# The Earth's Hemispheres

The Earth is shaped like a sphere. It can be divided into two halves. Each half is called a hemisphere. Hemisphere means "half a ball." The imaginary line that cuts the Earth in half is the equator. It runs around the middle of the Earth. Each half has a pole, the North Pole and the South Pole. They are opposite each other.

The seasons change when the Earth revolves around the sun. It is summer in the Northern Hemisphere when the Earth's axis is tilted toward the sun. When the Earth's axis is pointed away from the sun, it is summer in the Southern Hemisphere. The seasons are always opposite in the two hemispheres. December is winter in the United States, but it is summer in Australia. July is South Africa's winter, but England's summer.

### The Earth's Hemispheres

❶

| | |
|---|---|
| The Earth is shaped like a sphere. It can be divided into two | 13 |
| halves. Each half is called a hemisphere. Hemisphere means | 22 |
| "half a ball." The imaginary line that cuts the Earth in half is the | 36 |
| equator. It runs around the middle of the Earth. Each half has a | 49 |
| pole, the North Pole and the South Pole. They are opposite each | 61 |
| other. | 62 |
| The seasons change when the Earth revolves around the sun. | 72 |
| It is summer in the Northern Hemisphere when the Earth's axis | 83 |
| is tilted toward the sun. When the Earth's axis is pointed away | 95 |
| from the sun, it is summer in the Southern Hemisphere. The | 106 |
| seasons are always opposite in the two hemispheres. December | 115 |
| is winter in the United States, but it is summer in Australia. | 127 |
| July is South Africa's winter, but England's summer. | 135 |

❷ (in paragraph 1, after "Each half has a")

❸ (in paragraph 2, before "is winter in the United States")

)8100

Total Words Read _____  _____  _____

Errors Counted _____  _____  _____

WCPM ☐  ☐  ☐

| Norm Group Percentile from Table 2, page 6 | ☐ 90 | ☐ 90 | ☐ 90 |
|---|---|---|---|
| | ☐ 75 | ☐ 75 | ☐ 75 |
| | ☐ 50 | ☐ 50 | ☐ 50 |
| | ☐ 25 | ☐ 25 | ☐ 25 |
| | ☐ 10 | ☐ 10 | ☐ 10 |

Date _____  _____  _____

_____ ❶ What is the earth shaped like? (a sphere)

_____ ❷ What are the names of the two poles? (the North Pole and the South Pole)

_____ ❸ What season is December in the United States? (winter)

| | Seldom Weak Poor | | Always Strong Excellent |
|---|---|---|---|
| Phrasing | ├——————┼——————┤ | | |
| Expression | ├——————┼——————┤ | | |
| Punctuation | ├——————┼——————┤ | | |
| Rate | ├——————┼——————┤ | | |

Milk

Milk is produced by female mammals to feed their young. Ninety percent of milk comes from cows. A cow can give 200,000 glasses of milk during her lifetime. Some people also use milk from the goat, buffalo, camel, mare, llama, and zebra.

Milk goes through two processes to prepare it for sale. The first process breaks up the butterfat. This prevents the cream from separating and rising to the top. Milk is also sterilized. This kills the bacteria. It is safer to drink and stays fresh longer.

Milk is good for you. It has many essentials for a healthy body. These include protein, fat, sugar, salt, and vitamins A, C, and D. Milk is a major source of calcium. People should have three servings of milk products a day. Cheese, pudding, yogurt, and ice cream are all good sources of milk. Try some milk products today.

## Milk

| | 1st | 2nd | 3rd |
|---|---|---|---|

Milk is produced by female mammals to feed their young. ❶    10

Ninety percent of milk comes from cows. A cow can give    21

200,000 glasses of milk during her lifetime. Some people also    31

use milk from the goat, buffalo, camel, mare, llama, and zebra.    42

Milk goes through two processes to prepare it for sale. The    53

first process breaks up the butterfat. This prevents the cream from    64

separating and rising to the top. Milk is also sterilized. ❷ This kills    76

the bacteria. It is safer to drink and stays fresh longer.    87

Milk is good for you. It has many essentials for a healthy body.    100

These include protein, fat, sugar, salt, and vitamins A, C, and D.    112

Milk is a major source of calcium. ❸ People should have three    123

servings of milk products a day. Cheese, pudding, yogurt, and    133

ice cream are all good sources of milk. Try some milk products    145

today.    146

$\overline{)8760}$

❶ What percentage of milk comes from cows? (ninety percent)

❷ How is milk prepared to sell? (breaking up the butter fat; sterilizing the milk)

❸ Why should people drink milk? (has essentials for a healthy body; has protein, fat, sugar, salt, vitamins, calcium [any 2])

| | 1st | 2nd | 3rd |
|---|---|---|---|
| Total Words Read | | | |
| Errors Counted | | | |
| WCPM | | | |
| Norm Group Percentile from Table 2, page 6 | ❑ 90<br>❑ 75<br>❑ 50<br>❑ 25<br>❑ 10 | ❑ 90<br>❑ 75<br>❑ 50<br>❑ 25<br>❑ 10 | ❑ 90<br>❑ 75<br>❑ 50<br>❑ 25<br>❑ 10 |
| Date | | | |

| | Seldom<br>Weak<br>Poor | | Always<br>Strong<br>Excellent |
|---|---|---|---|
| Phrasing | ⊢ | ┼ | ⊣ |
| Expression | ⊢ | ┼ | ⊣ |
| Punctuation | ⊢ | ┼ | ⊣ |
| Rate | ⊢ | ┼ | ⊣ |

The Uncommon, Common Pet

Goldfish are the most common household pets in the entire world. Actually, there's nothing common about goldfish. The origins of goldfish begin in China. They were the first fish to become pets. Chinese monks kept them as decorations over 3000 years ago. Now there are more than 125 known varieties of goldfish.

The name "goldfish" came from a mutation. They were originally green, but their color changed. The fish became the bright orange color we know today. Fins often mutate or change. Long flowing fins, double fins, and absent dorsal fins are all mutations. Eye mutations also occur. "Telescope eyes" means the eyes of the fish stick out of their heads. Bubble-eyed goldfish have large sacks under their eyes. Remember, not all goldfish are gold. One popular kind of goldfish is black. Goldfish can be spotted, white, brown, yellow, or blue. It's easy to see why goldfish are such a common and popular pet. Perhaps you have had a goldfish as a pet.

The Uncommon, Common Pet

Goldfish are the most common household pets in the entire ❶
world. Actually, there's nothing common about goldfish. The
origins of goldfish begin in China. ❷ They were the first fish to
become pets. Chinese monks kept them as decorations over
3000 years ago. Now there are more than 125 known varieties
of goldfish.

The name "goldfish" came from a mutation. They were
originally green, but their color changed. The fish became the
bright orange color we know today. Fins often mutate or change.
Long flowing fins, double fins, and absent dorsal fins are all
mutations. Eye mutations also occur. "Telescope eyes" means the
eyes of the fish stick out of their heads. Bubble-eyed goldfish
have large sacks under their eyes. Remember, not all goldfish are
gold. One popular kind of goldfish is black. Goldfish can be
spotted, white, brown, yellow, or blue. ❸ It's easy to see why
goldfish are such a common and popular pet. Perhaps you have
had a goldfish as a pet.

| | 1st | 2nd | 3rd |
|---|---|---|---|
| 10 | | | |
| 18 | | | |
| 30 | | | |
| 39 | | | |
| 50 | | | |
| 52 | | | |
| 61 | | | |
| 71 | | | |
| 82 | | | |
| 93 | | | |
| 102 | | | |
| 113 | | | |
| 124 | | | |
| 135 | | | |
| 146 | | | |
| 157 | | | |
| 163 | | | |

| | 1st | 2nd | 3rd |
|---|---|---|---|
| Total Words Read | | | |
| Errors Counted | | | |
| WCPM | | | |

$)\overline{9780}$

|  | 1st | 2nd | 3rd |
|---|---|---|---|
| Norm Group Percentile from Table 2, page 6 | ❏ 90 | ❏ 90 | ❏ 90 |
| | ❏ 75 | ❏ 75 | ❏ 75 |
| | ❏ 50 | ❏ 50 | ❏ 50 |
| | ❏ 25 | ❏ 25 | ❏ 25 |
| | ❏ 10 | ❏ 10 | ❏ 10 |

Date ____ ____ ____

_____ ❶ What are the most common pets in the
world? (goldfish)

_____ ❷ Where do goldfish come from? (China)

_____ ❸ How are goldfish different from each
other? (fin mutation; color mutation;
eye mutation [any 2])

| | Seldom Weak Poor | | Always Strong Excellent |
|---|---|---|---|
| Phrasing | ├——————— | ———————— | ———————┤ |
| Expression | ├——————— | ———————— | ———————┤ |
| Punctuation | ├——————— | ———————— | ———————┤ |
| Rate | ├——————— | ———————— | ———————┤ |

Adapted from Pflaumer, S. (April 21, 2004). *Goldfish are more diverse than any other fish species.* DeKalb, IL: The Midweek.
Adapted from Goldfish. Britannica Conscise Encyclopedia. Retrieved May 29, 2004, from Encyclopedia Britannica Premium
Service. http://www.britannica.com/cbc/article?eu=391099. Adapted from information found at the following web pages:
www.petlibrary.com/goldfish/goldfish.html. www.kokosgoldfish.com. From Jerry L. Johns and Roberta L. Berglund, *Fluency:
Strategies & Assessments* (3rd ed.). Copyright © 2006 Kendall/Hunt Publishing Company (1-800-247-3458, ext. 4 or 5). May be
reproduced for noncommercial educational purposes.

### Nashville's Music

Country and western is an original American music style. It was first sung by settlers in the eastern mountains. It was born of hard work, strong emotion, and the love of a good story. Country and western music is loved by people from all walks of life. People identify with the songs as they relate to everyday life. Some people find country music sad. Songs often are about heartbreak, poverty, and homesickness. Other songs tell inspiring stories about freedom, peace, and love.

Nashville is country and western music's hometown. Hopeful musicians go to Nashville to become stars. It has the best recording studios. The Grand Ole Opry is Nashville's center stage. Many famous entertainers have performed there. On Saturday nights, you can hear a broadcast from its stage. The Grand Ole Opry also has an amusement park. Visitors like to go there. The Country Music Hall of Fame and Museum would be out of place in any other city. Country and western music fans hope that Nashville never stops producing new songs.

**Reading and Miscues Counted as Errors**

| | 1st | 2nd | 3rd |
|---|---|---|---|

### Nashville's Music

Country and western is an original American music style. It ❶ [10]
was first sung by settlers in the eastern mountains. It was born [22]
of hard work, strong emotion, and the love of a good story. [34]
Country and western music is loved by people from all walks of [46]
life. People identify with the songs as they relate to everyday life. [58]
Some people find country music sad. Songs often are about [68]
heartbreak, poverty, and homesickness. Other songs tell inspiring [76]
stories about freedom, peace, and love. ❷ [82]

Nashville is country and western music's hometown. Hopeful [90]
musicians go to Nashville to become stars. ❸ It has the best [101]
recording studios. The Grand Ole Opry is Nashville's center [110]
stage. Many famous entertainers have performed there. On [118]
Saturday nights, you can hear a broadcast from its stage. The [129]
Grand Ole Opry also has an amusement park. Visitors like to go [141]
there. The Country Music Hall of Fame and Museum would be [152]
out of place in any other city. Country and western music fans [164]
hope that Nashville never stops producing new songs. [172]

$$\overline{)10{,}320}$$

Total Words Read

Errors Counted

WCPM

| Norm Group Percentile from Table 2, page 6 | ❏ 90 ❏ 75 ❏ 50 ❏ 25 ❏ 10 | ❏ 90 ❏ 75 ❏ 50 ❏ 25 ❏ 10 | ❏ 90 ❏ 75 ❏ 50 ❏ 25 ❏ 10 |
|---|---|---|---|

Date ____

| | Seldom Weak Poor | | Always Strong Excellent |
|---|---|---|---|
| Phrasing | ├─── | ───┼─── | ───┤ |
| Expression | ├─── | ───┼─── | ───┤ |
| Punctuation | ├─── | ───┼─── | ───┤ |
| Rate | ├─── | ───┼─── | ───┤ |

_____ ❶ Where did country and western music originate? (America; eastern mountains)

_____ ❷ What kinds of stories does country and western music tell? (stories of heartbreak, poverty, homesickness, hard work, inspiration [any 2])

_____ ❸ Why do musicians go to Nashville? (to become stars)

Ronald Reagan, An American Hero

In 1911, Ronald Reagan was born in a small town in Illinois. He played football in high school. He saved many lives as a lifeguard on the Rock River. With humble beginnings, his life led him to achieve the great American dream.

His first job out of college was announcing Chicago Cubs baseball games on the radio. This job took him to California where he became a movie star. As president of the Screen Actor's Guild, he drew national attention. He also met Nancy Davis, who he married.

In 1966, he won California's governor's seat. Then in 1980 he became the Fortieth President of the United States. As president, he faced many personal and national difficulties with humor and honor. After he was shot in 1981, he joked to his wife, "Honey, I forgot to duck." When the nation went into deep recession, he urged people to be brave. He asked them to think about future generations rather than short-term comforts. Reagan thought his greatest presidential contribution was the peaceful end of the Cold War. He was loved by many. He will be remembered as a true American hero.

### Ronald Reagan, An American Hero

In 1911, Ronald Reagan was born in a small town in Illinois. He played football in high school. He save many lives as a lifeguard on the Rock River. With humble beginnings, his life led him to achieve the great American dream.

His first job out of college was announcing Chicago Cubs baseball games on the radio. This job took him to California where he became a movie star. As president of the Screen Actor's Guild, he drew national attention. He also met Nancy Davis, who he married.

In 1966, he won California's governor's seat. Then in 1980 he became the Fortieth President of the United States. As president, he faced many personal and national difficulties with humor and honor. After he was shot in 1981, he joked to his wife, "Honey, I forgot to duck." When the nation went into deep recession, he urged people to be brave. He asked them to think about future generations rather than short-term comforts. Reagan thought his greatest presidential contribution was the peaceful end of the Cold War. He was loved by many. He will be remembered as a true American hero.

| | 1st | 2nd | 3rd |
|---|---|---|---|
| 12 | | | |
| 24 | | | |
| 34 | | | |
| 42 | | | |
| 52 | | | |
| 63 | | | |
| 74 | | | |
| 83 | | | |
| 88 | | | |
| 98 | | | |
| 108 | | | |
| 117 | | | |
| 130 | | | |
| 142 | | | |
| 154 | | | |
| 162 | | | |
| 170 | | | |
| 183 | | | |
| 189 | | | |
| Total Words Read | | | |
| Errors Counted | | | |
| WCPM | | | |

Norm Group Percentile from Table 2, page 6

| | 1st | 2nd | 3rd |
|---|---|---|---|
| | ❑ 90 | ❑ 90 | ❑ 90 |
| | ❑ 75 | ❑ 75 | ❑ 75 |
| | ❑ 50 | ❑ 50 | ❑ 50 |
| | ❑ 25 | ❑ 25 | ❑ 25 |
| | ❑ 10 | ❑ 10 | ❑ 10 |

Date _____ _____ _____

$\overline{)11,340}$

_____ ❶ What did Ronald Reagan do as a young man? (he played football; he was a life-guard; he announced baseball games on the radio; he was a movie star [any 2])

_____ ❷ Besides President, what is another office Ronald Reagan held? (Screen Actor's Guild president; Governor of California)

_____ ❸ How did he handle difficulty as president? (with humor; with honor; joking with Nancy "Honey, I forgot to duck;" asking people to think of the long-term effects of their choices)

| | Seldom Weak Poor | | Always Strong Excellent |
|---|---|---|---|
| Phrasing | ⊢ | ┼ | ⊣ |
| Expression | ⊢ | ┼ | ⊣ |
| Punctuation | ⊢ | ┼ | ⊣ |
| Rate | ⊢ | ┼ | ⊣ |

Adapted from articles at www.msnbc.com *President Reagan dies; It's a sad day for America. Bush says; Ronald Reagan, 1911–2004; One for "The Gipper."* From Jerry L. Johns and Roberta L. Berglund, *Fluency: Strategies & Assessments* (3rd ed.).

Ballet

A ballerina is a performing artist and an extremely disciplined athlete. She embodies strength and beauty. She is the star of the performance. Ballets such as The Nutcracker, Swan Lake, and Sleeping Beauty are timeless classics. The charming dancers make the stories come alive. These stories resonate with romantics of every age.

Ballet became a distinct dance form over 500 years ago in Italy. Ballet's first centuries were spent as courtly entertainment. France's Royal Ballet Academy was founded in 1661. This, and other performing arts schools, helped open ballet to women. Prior to this time period, all ballet dancers were men. Boys wore wigs and masks to dance female roles. Ballet was also opened to the public. The first public performances were in 1708.

Public performances and female dancers renewed ballet. Ballet went through numerous changes in the next century. Dancers began dancing on their toes. Their traditional heavy skirts hindered their dancing. One dancer tried a flimsy, short skirt. This "tutu" became ballet's trademark. The star ballerina we know today was born. People loved the graceful dancers. Ballet dancers bring fancy and drama together in a unique and engaging way. Together, these aspects make ballet one of the world's most popular art forms.

## Ballet

A ballerina is a performing artist and an extremely disciplined athlete. She embodies strength and beauty. She is the star of the ❶ performance. Ballets such as The Nutcracker, Swan Lake, and Sleeping Beauty are timeless classics. The charming dancers make the stories come alive. These stories resonate with romantics of every age.

Ballet became a distinct dance form over 500 years ago in Italy. Ballet's first centuries were spent as courtly entertainment. France's Royal Ballet Academy was founded in 1661. This, and other performing arts schools, helped open ballet to women. Prior to this time period, all ballet dancers were men. Boys wore wigs and masks to dance female roles. ❷ Ballet was also opened to the public. The first public performances were in 1708.

Public performances and female dancers renewed ballet. Ballet went through numerous changes in the next century. Dancers began dancing on their toes. Their traditional heavy skirts hindered their dancing. ❸ One dancer tried a flimsy, short skirt. This "tutu" became ballet's trademark. The star ballerina we know today was born. People loved the graceful dancers. Ballet dancers bring fancy and drama together in a unique and engaging way. Together, these aspects make ballet one of the world's most popular art forms.

| | 1st | 2nd | 3rd |
|---|---|---|---|
| 10 | ——— | ——— | ——— |
| 22 | ——— | ——— | ——— |
| 31 | ——— | ——— | ——— |
| 39 | ——— | ——— | ——— |
| 48 | ——— | ——— | ——— |
| 52 | ——— | ——— | ——— |
| 63 | ——— | ——— | ——— |
| 72 | ——— | ——— | ——— |
| 82 | ——— | ——— | ——— |
| 92 | ——— | ——— | ——— |
| 104 | ——— | ——— | ——— |
| 116 | ——— | ——— | ——— |
| 124 | ——— | ——— | ——— |
| 132 | ——— | ——— | ——— |
| 141 | ——— | ——— | ——— |
| 150 | ——— | ——— | ——— |
| 160 | ——— | ——— | ——— |
| 169 | ——— | ——— | ——— |
| 179 | ——— | ——— | ——— |
| 189 | ——— | ——— | ——— |
| 199 | ——— | ——— | ——— |
| 204 | ——— | ——— | ——— |

$\overline{)12{,}240}$

| | 1st | 2nd | 3rd |
|---|---|---|---|
| Total Words Read | ——— | ——— | ——— |
| Errors Counted | ——— | ——— | ——— |
| WCPM | ☐ | ☐ | ☐ |

Norm Group Percentile from Table 2, page 6

| 1st | 2nd | 3rd |
|---|---|---|
| ❏ 90 | ❏ 90 | ❏ 90 |
| ❏ 75 | ❏ 75 | ❏ 75 |
| ❏ 50 | ❏ 50 | ❏ 50 |
| ❏ 25 | ❏ 25 | ❏ 25 |
| ❏ 10 | ❏ 10 | ❏ 10 |

Date ——— ——— ———

| | Seldom Weak Poor | | Always Strong Excellent |
|---|---|---|---|
| Phrasing | ├ | ┼ | ┤ |
| Expression | ├ | ┼ | ┤ |
| Punctuation | ├ | ┼ | ┤ |
| Rate | ├ | ┼ | ┤ |

_____ ❶ How can a ballerina be described? (a performing artist; a disciplined athlete; strong; beautiful; star)

_____ ❷ Before women danced ballet, who danced female roles? (men; boys dressed in wigs and masks)

_____ ❸ Why did ballet dancers start wearing the tutu? (the heavy skirts hindered their dancing)

# Resources for Fluency Checks

# Class Fluency Record— Primary Grades

Teacher _____ Grade _____

Date _____    Date _____    Date _____

Passage _____    Passage _____    Passage _____

```
─180                    ─180                    ─180
─170                    ─170                    ─170
─160                    ─160                    ─160
─150                    ─150                    ─150
─140                    ─140                    ─140
─130                    ─130                    ─130
─120                    ─120                    ─120
─110                    ─110                    ─110
─100                    ─100                    ─100
─90                     ─90                     ─90
─80                     ─80                     ─80
─70                     ─70                     ─70
─60                     ─60                     ─60
─50                     ─50                     ─50
─40                     ─40                     ─40
─30                     ─30                     ─30
─≤20                    ─≤20                    ─≤20
```

# Class Fluency
## Record—Upper Grades

Teacher _____   Grade _____

Date _____   Date _____   Date _____

Passage _____   Passage _____   Passage _____

| | | |
|---|---|---|
| —220— | —220— | —220— |
| —210— | —210— | —210— |
| —200— | —200— | —200— |
| —190— | —190— | —190— |
| —180— | —180— | —180— |
| —170— | —170— | —170— |
| —160— | —160— | —160— |
| —150— | —150— | —150— |
| —140— | —140— | —140— |
| —130— | —130— | —130— |
| —120— | —120— | —120— |
| —110— | —110— | —110— |
| —100— | —100— | —100— |
| —90— | —90— | —90— |
| —80— | —80— | —80— |
| —70— | —70— | —70— |
| —60— | —60— | —60— |
| —≤50— | —≤50— | —≤50— |

# 4-Point Fluency Rubric for Oral Reading

Student _____ Selection _____ Level _____ Date _____

| FOCUS | 1 | 2 | 3 | 4 |
|---|---|---|---|---|
| **Rate** | Slow and laborious Struggles with words | Rate varies Some hesitations | Generally conversational Some smooth, some choppy | Conversational and consistent Smooth and fluent throughout |
| **Expression** | Monotone | Monotone combined with some expression | Appropriate expression used much of the time | Appropriate expression maintained throughout |
| **Phrasing** | Word-by-word Long pauses between words | Some word-by-word, some phrases | Mostly phrases, some smooth, some choppy | Phrases consistently throughout, generally smooth and fluent |
| **Punctuation** | Little or no use | Uses some Ignores some | Uses most of the time | Uses consistently throughout |

**Suggestions for Rubric Use:**

You may wish to choose one area for assessing a student's progress (for example, rate, expression, phrasing, or punctuation), or you may wish to score a student's reading in all four areas. If you wish to score a student's multiple readings of a selection, you may wish to highlight each reading with a different color. For example, after the first reading, circle the words for the score for each area you are checking in yellow. The next time you check the student on the same passage, use a blue highlighter, and the third time a green highlighter to check (✓) your ratings. You and the student can easily see if progress is being made in one or several areas as a result of the multiple re-readings.

Record your color-coding below.

First reading _____

Second reading _____

Third reading _____

From Jerry L. Johns and Roberta L. Berglund, *Fluency: Strategies & Assessments* (3rd ed.). Copyright © 2006 Kendall/Hunt Publishing Company (1-800-247-3458, ext. 4 or 5). May be reproduced for noncommercial educational purposes.

# Holistic Oral Reading Fluency Scale
## National Assessment of Educational Progress (NAEP)

**Level 4**   Reads primarily in larger, meaningful phrase groups. Although some regressions, repetitions, and deviations from text may be present, these do not detract from the overall structure of the story. Preservation of the author's syntax is consistent. Some or most of the story is read with expressive interpretation.

**Level 3**   Reads primarily in three-or-four word phrase groups. Some small groupings may be present. However, the majority of the phrasing seems appropriate and preserves the syntax of the author. Little or no expressive interpretation is present.

**Level 2**   Reads primarily in two-word phrases with some three-or-four word groupings. Some word-by-word reading may be present. Word groupings may seem awkward and unrelated to larger context of sentence or passage.

**Level 1**   Reads primarily word-by-word. Occasional two-word or three-word phrases may occur—but these are infrequent and/or they do not preserve meaningful syntax.

From Jerry L. Johns and Roberta L. Berglund, *Fluency: Strategies & Assessments* (3rd ed.). Copyright © 2006 Kendall/Hunt Publishing Company (1-800-247-3458, ext. 4 or 5). May be reproduced for noncommercial educational purposes.

U.S. Department of Education, National Center for Education Statistics (1995). *Listening to children read aloud, 15.* Washington, DC: U.S. Department of Education.

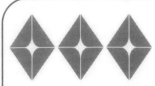 **Cumulative Record for Fluency Checks**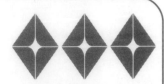

| GRADE | DATE _____ FIRST READING | | | DATE _____ SECOND READING | | | DATE _____ THIRD READING | | |
|---|---|---|---|---|---|---|---|---|---|
| | WCPM | Comp. | Exp. | WCPM | Comp. | Exp. | WCPM | Comp. | Exp. |
| **1** ___ Teacher | | | | | | | | | |
| **2** ___ Teacher | | | | | | | | | |
| **3** ___ Teacher | | | | | | | | | |
| **4** ___ Teacher | | | | | | | | | |
| **5** ___ Teacher | | | | | | | | | |
| **6** ___ Teacher | | | | | | | | | |
| **7** ___ Teacher | | | | | | | | | |
| **8** ___ Teacher | | | | | | | | | |

WCPM = Words Correct Per Minute
Comp. = Comprehension (Good, Fair, Poor based on your judgment)
Exp. = Expression (Good, Fair, Poor or use rubric on page 160)

# Appendix

## Answers to Anticipation Guide for Fluency

◇◇◇ **Directions** ◇◇◇

Compare our notes to your initial impressions on the Anticipation Guide on page 2.

|   |   | **AFTER READING** | |  |
|---|---|---|---|---|
| | | **T or F** | **Page(s)** | **Question(s)** |
| 1. | Fluency in reading is most relevant at the beginning stages of reading. | F | 4, 5, 15 | 2, 3, 5, 9 |
| 2. | Fluency is independent of comprehension. | F | 3 | 1 |
| 3. | Research has identified several methods to increase reading fluency. | T | 16, 17 | 10, 11 |
| 4. | Oral reading fluency is developed best through independent reading. | F | 16, 17 | 10 |
| 5. | One aspect of fluency can be judged by determining the student's rate of reading in words per minute (WPM). | T | 4, 5, 9 | 4, 7 |
| 6. | It is appropriate to consider fluency in silent reading. | T | 3, 4 | 1, 3 |
| 7. | Fluency is actually speed of reading. | F | 3 | 1 |
| 8. | Fluency strategies are primarily for students experiencing difficulty in reading. | F | 18 | 12 |
| 9. | Students should adjust reading rate according to their purposes for reading. | T | 4, 8 | 2, 3, 6 |
| 10. | A reasonable oral fluency rate for third-grade students is 160 words correct per minute (WCPM) by the end of the school year. | F | 5 | 5 |
| 11. | Round-robin oral reading is an effective fluency activity. | F | 13 | 8 |

# References

Adams, M. J. (1990). *Beginning to read: Thinking and learning about print.* Cambridge, MA: MIT Press.

Allington, R. L. (1983a). Fluency: The neglected reading goal. *The Reading Teacher, 36,* 556–561.

Allington, R. L. (1983b). The reading instruction provided readers of differing abilities. *Elementary School Journal, 83,* 548–559.

Allington, R. L. (2001). *What really matters for struggling readers: Designing research-based programs.* New York: Longman.

Allington, R. L. (2006). Fluency: Still waiting after all these years. In S. J. Samuels & A.E. Farstrup (Eds.), *What research has to say about fluency instruction* (pp. 94–105). Newark, DE: International Reading Association.

Anderson, C. A. (2000). Sustained silent reading: Try it, you'll like it. *The Reading Teacher, 54,* 258–259.

Anderson, R. C., Hiebert, E. H., Scott, J. A., & Wilkinson, I. A. G. (1985). *Becoming a nation of readers: The report of the Commission on Reading.* Washington, DC: The National Institute of Education.

Armbruster, B. B., Lehr, F., & Osborn, J. (2001). *Put reading first: The research building blocks for teaching children to read.* Jessup, MD: National Institute for Literacy.

Ash, G. E. (2006). Meaningful oral and silent reading in the elementary and middle school classroom. In T. Rasinski, C. Blachowicz, & K. Lems (Eds.), *Fluency instruction: Research-based best practices* (pp. 155–172). New York: Guilford.

Bear, D. R., & Barone, D. (1998). *Developing literacy: An integrated approach to assessment and instruction.* Boston: Houghton Mifflin.

Beck, I., & McKeown, M. (1981). Developing questions that promote comprehension: The story map. *Language Arts, 58,* 913–918.

Behavioral Research and Teaching. (2005). *Oral reading fluency: 90 years of measurement* (Technical Report No.33). Eugene, OR: Author.

Berglund, R. L. (1988). Shared book experience: Bridging the gap between lap reading and school reading. *Wisconsin State Reading Association Journal, 31,* 23–32.

Berglund, R. L., & Johns, J. L. (1983). A primer on uninterrupted sustained silent reading. *The Reading Teacher, 36,* 534–539.

Betts, E. A. (1946). *Foundations of reading instruction.* New York: American Book Company.

Blachman, B. A. (2000). Phonological awareness in M. L. Kamil, P. B. Mosenthal, P. D. Pearson, & R. Barr. (Eds.). *Handbook of Reading Research, Vol. III,* 483–502. Mahwah, NJ: Erlbaum.

Blachowicz, C. L. Z., Sullivan, D. M., & Cieply, C. (2001). Fluency snapshots: A quick screening tool for your classroom. *Reading Psychology, 22,* 95–109.

Bradley, L., & Bryant, P. (1983). Categorizing sounds and learning to read: A causal connection. *Nature, 30,* 419–421.

Breznitz, Z. (2006). *Fluency in reading: Synchronization of processes.* Mahwah, NJ: Erlbaum.

Burns, B. (2001). *Guided reading: A how-to for all grades.* Arlington Heights, IL: SkyLight.

Burns, M. S., Griffin, P., & Snow, C. E. (Eds.) (1999). *Starting out right: A guide to promoting children's reading success.* Washington, DC: National Academy Press.

Butler, A., & Turbill, J. (1985). *Towards a reading-writing classroom.* Portsmouth, NH: Heinemann.

Byrne, B., & Fielding-Barnsley, R. (1993). Evaluation of a program to teach phonemic awareness to young children; A 1-year follow-up. *Journal of Educational Psychology, 83,* 451–455.

Carbo, M. (1978). Teaching reading with talking books. *The Reading Teacher, 32,* 267–273.

Carbo, M. (1981). Making books talk to children. *The Reading Teacher, 35,* 186–189.

Carnine, D. W., Silbert, J., Kame'enui, E. J., & Tarver, S. G. (2004). *Direct instruction reading* (4th ed.). Upper Saddle River, NJ: Pearson.

Carver, R. P. (1989). Silent reading rates in grade equivalents. *Journal of Reading Behavior, 21,* 155–166.

Cassidy, J., & Cassidy, D. (2005/2006). What's hot, what's not for 2006. *Reading Today, 23*(3), 1, 8–9.

Corso, L., Funk, S., & Gaffney, J. (2001/2002). An educational evening out. *The Reading Teacher, 55,* 326–329.

Cromer, W. (1970). The difference model: A new explanation for some reading difficulties. *Journal of Educational Psychology, 61,* 471–483.

Cunningham, A. E. (1990). Explicit versus implicit instruction in phonemic awareness. *Journal of Experimental Child Psychology, 50,* 429–444.

Cunningham, P. M., & Hall, D. P. (1994a). *Making big words: Multilevel, hands-on spelling and phonics activities.* Parsippany, NJ: Good Apple.

Cunningham, P. M., & Hall, D. P. (1994b). *Making words: Multilevel, hands-on, developmentally appropriate spelling and phonics activities.* Parsippany, NJ: Good Apple.

Cunningham, P. M., & Hall, D. P. (1997a). *Making more words: Multilevel, hands-on phonics and spelling activities.* Torrence, CA: Good Apple.

Cunningham, P. M., Hall, D. P. (1997b). *Month-by-month phonics for first grade.* Greensboro, NC: Carson-Dellosa.

Cunningham, P. M., & Hall, D. P. (1998). *Month-by-month phonics for upper grades: A second chance for struggling readers and students learning English.* Greensboro, NC: Carson-Dellosa.

Cunningham, P. M. (1999). *The teacher's guide to the four blocks.* Greensboro, NC: Carson-Dellosa.

Dowhower, S. L. (1987). Effects of repeated reading on second-grade transitional readers' fluency and comprehension. *Reading Research Quarterly, 22,* 389–406.

Dowhower, S. L. (1991). Speaking of prosody: Fluency's unattended bedfellow. *Theory Into Practice, 30,* 165–175.

Ehri, L., Nunes, S. R., Willows, D. M., Schuster, B. V., Yaghoub-Zadeh, Z., & Shanahan, T. (2001). Phonemic awareness instruction helps children learn to read: Evidence from the National Reading Panel's meta-analysis. *Reading Research Quarterly 36,* 250–287.

Eldredge, J. L., Reutzel, D. R., & Hollingsworth, P. M. (1996). Comparing the effectiveness of two oral reading practices: Round-robin reading and the shared book experience. *Journal of Literacy Research, 28,* 201–225.

Elish-Piper, L., Johns, J. L., & Davis, S. D. (2006). *Teaching reading Pre-K–grade 3* (3rd ed.). Dubuque, IA: Kendall/Hunt.

Elley, W. B. (1988). Vocabulary acquisition from listening to stories. *Reading Research Quarterly, 24,* 174–187.

Enz, B. (1989). *The 90 per cent success solution.* Paper presented at the International Reading Association annual convention, New Orleans.

Flynn, R. M. (2004/2005). Curriculum-based readers theatre: Setting the stage for reading and retention. *The Reading Teacher, 58,* 360–365.

Forman, J., & Sanders, M. E. (1998). *Project Leap First Grade Norming Study: 1993–1998.* Unpublished Manuscript.

Fountas, I. C., & Pinnell, G. S. (2000). *Matching books to readers: Using leveled books in guided reading, K-3.* Portsmouth, NH: Heinemann.

Fountas, I. C., & Pinnell, G. S. (2001). *Guiding readers and writers: Grades 3–6.* Portsmouth, NH: Heinemann.

Fox, B. J. (2004). *Word identification strategies* (3rd ed.). Columbus: Merrill.

Fry, E. (1968). A readability formula that saves time. *Journal of Reading, 11,* 513–516.

Fry, E. (1977). Fry's readability graph: Clarifications, validity, and extension to level 17. *Journal of Reading, 21,* 242–252.

Gillet, J. W., Temple, C., & Crawford, A. N. (2004). *Understanding reading problems: Assessment and instruction* (6th ed.). Boston: Allyn and Bacon.

Greene, F. (1979). Radio reading. In C. Pennock (Ed.), *Reading comprehension at four linguistic levels* (pp. 104–107). Newark, DE: International Reading Association.

Gunning, T. G. (2000). *Best books for building literacy for elementary school children.* Boston: Allyn and Bacon.

Gunning, T. G. (2005). *Creating literacy instruction for all students* (5th ed.). Boston: Allyn and Bacon.

Harris, T. L., & Hodges, R. E. (Eds.) (1995). *The literacy dictionary: The vocabulary of reading and writing.* Newark, DE: International Reading Association.

Hasbrouck, J. E., & Tindal, G. (1992). Curriculum-based oral reading fluency norms for students in grades 2 through 5. *Teaching Exceptional Children, 24,* 41–44.

Hasbrouck, J., & Tindal, G. A. (2006). Oral reading fluency norms: A valuable assessment tool for reading teachers. *The Reading Teacher, 59,* 636–644.

Heckelman, R. G. (1969). A neurological-impress method of remedial-reading instruction. *Academic Therapy Quarterly, 4,* 277–282.

Heilman, A. W., Blair, T. R., & Rupley, W. H. (2002). *Principles and practices of teaching reading* (10th ed.). Upper Saddle River, NJ: Merrill Prentice-Hall.

Herrell, A. L. (2000). *Fifty strategies for teaching English language learners.* Upper Saddle River, NJ: Prentice-Hall.

Hoffman, J. V. (1987). Rethinking the role of oral reading in basal instruction. *Elementary School Journal, 87,* 367–373.

Hohn, W. & Ehri, L. (1983). Do alphabet letters help prereaders acquire phonemic segmentation skills? *Journal of Educational Psychology, 75,* 752–762.

Holdaway, D. (1979). *The foundations of literacy.* Portsmouth, NH: Heinemann.

Howe, K. B., & Shinn, M. M. (2001). *Standard reading assessment passages (RAPS) for use in general outcome measurement: A manual describing development and technical features.* Eden Prairie, MN: Edformation.

Hudson, R. F., Lane, H. B., & Pullen, P. C. (2005). Reading fluency assessment: What, why, and how? *The Reading Teacher, 58,* 702–714.

Hunt, L. C., Jr. (1970). The effect of self-selection, interest, and motivation on independent, instructional, and frustrational levels. *The Reading Teacher, 24,* 146–151, 158.

Hyatt, A. V. (1943). *The place of oral reading in the school program: Its history and development from 1880–1941.* New York: Teachers College Press.

Indiana Library Federation (2001). Read-aloud books too good to miss. http://www.ilfonline.org/Programs/ReadAloud/readaloud.htm.

International Reading Association (2000). *Making a difference means making it different: A position statement of the International Reading Association.* Newark, DE: Author.

Johns, J. L. (1975). Dolch list of common nouns—A comparison. *The Reading Teacher, 28,* 338–340.

Johns, J. L. (1976). Updating the Dolch basic sight vocabulary. *Reading Horizons, 16,* 104–111.

Johns, J. L. (2005a). *Basic reading inventory* (9th ed.). Dubuque, IA: Kendall/Hunt.

Johns, J. L. (2005b). Fluency norms for students in grades one through eight. *Illinois Reading Council Journal, 33*(4), 3–8.

Johns, J. L., & Galen, N. (1977). Reading instruction in the middle 50's: What tomorrow's teachers remember today. *Reading Horizons, 17,* 251–254.

Johns, J. L., & Lenski, S. D. (2005). *Improving reading: Strategies and resources* (4th ed.). Dubuque, IA: Kendall/Hunt.

Johnson, L., Graham, S., & Harris, K. R. (1997). The effects of goal setting and self-instruction on learning a reading comprehension strategy: A study of students with learning disabilities. *Journal of Learning Disabilities, 30,* 80–90.

Keehn, S. (2003). The effect of instruction and practice through readers theatre on young readers' oral reading fluency. *Reading Research and Instruction, 42,* 40–61.

Keene, E. D., & Zimmermann, S. (1997). *Mosaic of thought.* Portsmouth, NH: Heinemann.

Klenk, L., & Kibby, M. L. (2000). Re-mediating reading difficulties: Appraising the past, reconciling the present, constructing the future. In M. L. Kamil, P. B. Mosenthal, P. D. Pearson, & R. Barr (Eds.), *Handbook of reading research* (Vol. III) (pp. 667–690). Mahwah, NJ: Erlbaum.

Krashen, S. D. (2004). *The power of reading: Insights from the research* (2nd ed.). Portsmouth, NH: Heinemann.

Kuhn, M. (2004/2005). Helping students become accurate, expressive readers: Fluency instruction for small groups. *The Reading Teacher, 58,* 338–344.

Kuhn, M. R., & Stahl, S. A. (2000). *Fluency: A review of developmental and remedial practices.* Ann Arbor, MI: Center for the Improvement of Early Reading Achievement.

Kuhn, M. R., & Stahl, S. A. (2004). Fluency: A review of developmental and remedial practices. In R. B. Ruddell & N. J. Unrau (Eds.), *Theoretical models and processes of reading* (5th ed.) (pp. 412–453). Newark, DE: International Reading Association.

LaBerge, D., & Samuels, S. J. (1974). Toward a theory of automatic information processing in reading. *Cognitive Psychology, 6,* 293–323.

Layne, S. L. (1996). *Vocabulary acquisition by fourth-grade students from listening to teachers' oral reading of novels.* Unpublished doctoral dissertation, Northern Illinois University, DeKalb.

Lundberg, I., Frost, J., & Petersen, O. P. (1988). Effects of an extensive program for stimulating phonological awareness in preschool children. *Reading Research Quarterly, 23,* 264–284.

Mallon, B., & Berglund, R. L. (1984). The language experience approach to reading: Recurring questions and their answers. *The Reading Teacher, 37,* 867–871.

Maro, N. (2001). Reading to improve fluency. *Illinois Reading Council Journal, 29*(3), 10–18.

Maro, N. (2004). *Personal communication,* August 13, 2004.

Martin, B., Jr. (1987). *Brown bear, brown bear, what do you see?* New York: Holt.

Martinez, M., Roser, N. L., & Strecker, S. (1998/1999). "I never thought I could be a star:" A Readers Theatre ticket to fluency. *The Reading Teacher, 52,* 326–334.

Miccinati, J. (1985). Using prosodic cues to teach oral reading fluency. *The Reading Teacher, 39,* 206–212.

Moskal, M. K. (2005/2006). Student self-selected repeated reading: Successful fluency development for disfluent readers. *Illinois Reading Council Journal, 34*(1), 3–11.

National Reading Panel (2000). *Teaching children to read: An evidenced-based assessment of the scientific research literature on reading and its implications for reading instruction.* Washington, DC: National Institute of Child Health & Human Development.

New Standards Primary Literacy Committee (1999). *Reading & writing grade by grade: Primary literacy standards for kindergarten through third grade.* Pittsburgh: National Center on Education and the Economy and the University of Pittsburgh.

Opitz, M. F., & Ford, M. P. (2001). *Reaching readers: Flexible & innovative strategies for guided reading.* Portsmouth, NH: Heinemann.

Opitz, M. F., & Rasinski, T. V. (1998). *Good-bye round robin: 25 effective oral reading strategies.* Portsmouth, NH: Heinemann.

O'Shea, L. J., & Sindelar, P. T. (1983). The effects of segmenting written discourse on the reading comprehension of low- and high-performance readers. *Reading Research Quarterly, 18,* 458–465.

O'Shea, L. J., Sindelar, P. T., & O'Shea, D. J. (1985). The effects of repeated readings and attentional cues on reading fluency and comprehension. *Journal of Reading Behavior, 17,* 129–142.

Pearson, P. D., & Fielding, L. (1991). Comprehension instruction. In R. Barr, M. L. Kamil, P. Mosenthal, & P. D. Pearson (Eds.), *Handbook of reading research* (Vol. II) (pp. 815–860). New York: Longman.

Person, M. E. (1993). Say it right! In M. W. Olson & S. P. Homan, (Eds.). *Teacher to teacher: Strategies for the elementary classroom* (pp. 37–38). Newark, DE: International Reading Association.

Pikulski, J. J., & Chard, D. J. (2005). Fluency: Bridge between decoding and reading comprehension. *The Reading Teacher, 58,* 510–519.

Pilgreen, J. (2000). *The SSR handbook: How to organize and manage a Sustained Silent Reading program.* Portsmouth, NH: Heinemann.

Pinnell, G. S., & Fountas, I. C. (2002). *Leveled books for readers, grades 3–6.* Portsmouth, NH: Heinemann.

Pinnell, G. S., Pikulski, J. J., Wixson, K. K., Campbell, J. R., Gough, P. B., & Beatty, A. S. (1995). *Listening to children read aloud.* Washington, DC: Office of Educational Research and Improvement, U.S. Department of Education.

Rasinski, T. (2002). Fluency. In B. J. Guzzetti (Ed.). *Literacy in America: An encyclopedia of history, theory, and practice* (Vol. 1) (pp. 191–193). Santa Barbara, CA: ABC-CLIO.

Rasinski, T. (2006). Reading fluency instruction: Moving beyond accuracy, automaticity, and prosody. *The Reading Teacher, 59,* 704–706.

Rasinski, T., & Padak, N. (1996). *Holistic reading strategies: Teaching students who find reading difficult.* Englewood Cliffs, NJ: Merrill.

Rasinski, T. V. (1990). Effects of repeated reading and listening-while-reading on reading fluency. *Journal of Educational Research, 83,* 147–150.

Rasinski, T. V. (2000). Speed does matter in reading. *The Reading Teacher, 54,* 146–151.

Rasinski, T. V., Padak, N. D., McKeon, C. A., Wilfong, L. G., Friedauer, J. A., & Heim, P. (2005). Is reading fluency a key for successful high school reading? *Journal of Adolescent & Adult Reading, 40,* 22–27.

Reutzel, D. R., & Hollingsworth, P. M. (1993). Effects of fluency training on second graders' reading comprehension. *Journal of Educational Research, 86,* 325–331.

Reutzel, D. R., Hollingsworth, P. M., & Eldredge, L. (1994). Oral reading instruction: The impact on student reading comprehension. *Journal of Educational Research, 86,* 325–331.

Roser, N. L. (2001). *Supporting the literacy of bilingual middle graders with culturally relevant readers theatre scripts.* Paper presented at the 46th Annual Convention of the International Reading Association, New Orleans, LA.

Routman, R. (2000). *Conversations: Strategies for teaching, learning, and evaluating.* Portsmouth, NH: Heinemann.

Samuels, S. J. (1979). The method of repeated readings. *The Reading Teacher, 32,* 403–408.

Samuels, S. J. (2002). Reading fluency: Its development and assessment. In A. E. Farstrup & S. J. Samuels (Eds.), *What research has to say about reading instruction* (3rd ed.) (pp. 166–183). Newark, DE: International Reading Association.

Samuels, S. J. (2006). Toward a model of reading fluency. In S. J. Samuels & A. E. Farstrup (Eds.), *What research has to say about fluency instruction* (pp. 24–46). Newark, DE: International Reading Association.

Searfoss, L. (1975). Radio reading. *The Reading Teacher, 29*, 295–296.

Shanahan, T. (2000a). *Literacy teaching framework.* Unpublished manuscript, University of Illinois at Chicago.

Shanahan, T. (2000b). *Teaching fluency in the high school.* Unpublished manuscript, University of Illinois at Chicago.

Shepard, A. (1997). *From stories to stage: Tips for reader's theatre.* http://www.aaronshep.com/rt/Tips3.

Sindelar, P. T., Monda, L. E., & O'Shea, L. J. (1990). Effects of repeated readings on instructional- and mastery-level readers. *Journal of Educational Research, 83*, 220–226.

Spache, G. D. (1953). A new readability formula for primary-grade reading materials. *The Elementary School Journal, 53*, 410–413.

Stanovich, K. E. (1986). Matthew effects in reading: Some consequences of individual differences in the acquisition of literacy. *Reading Research Quarterly, 21*, 360–407.

Stanovich, K. E. (1993). The language code: Issues in word recognition. In S. R. Yussen, & M. C. Smith (Eds.). *Reading across the life span* (pp. 111–135). Hillsdale, NJ: Erlbaum.

Stauffer, R. G. (1980). *The language-experience approach to the teaching of reading* (2nd ed.). New York: Harper & Row.

Strickland, D. S. (1993). Some tips for using big books. In M. W. Olson & S. P. Homan, (Eds.), *Teacher to Teacher: Strategies for the elementary classroom* (pp. 31–33). Newark, DE: International Reading Association.

Strickland, D. S., Ganske, K., & Monroe, J. K. (2002). *Supporting struggling readers and writers: Strategies for classroom intervention 3–6.* Newark, DE: International Reading Association.

Sullivan, J. (2004). *The children's literature lover's book of lists.* San Francisco: Jossey-Bass.

Teale, W. H., & Shanahan, T. (2001). Ignoring the essential: Myths about fluency. *Illinois Reading Council Journal, 29*(3), 5–8.

Topping, K. (1987a). Paired reading: A powerful technique for parent use. *The Reading Teacher, 40*, 608–614.

Topping, K. (1987b). Peer tutored paired reading: Outcome data from ten projects. *Educational Psychology, 7,* 604–614.

Topping, K. (1989). Peer tutoring and paired reading: Combining two powerful techniques. *The Reading Teacher, 42*, 488–494.

Topping, K. J. (2006). Building reading fluency: Cognitive, behavioral, and socioemotional factors and the role of peer-mediated learning. In S. J. Samuels & A. E. Farstrup (Eds.), *What research has to say about fluency instruction* (pp. 106–129). Newark, DE: International Reading Association.

Torgesen, J. K. (2004). Lessons learned from research on interventions for students who have difficulty learning to read. In P. McCardle & V. Chhabra (Eds.), *The voice of evidence in reading research* (pp. 355–382). Baltimore: Paul H. Brooks.

Torgesen, J. K., & Hudson, R. F. (2006). Reading fluency: Critical issues for readers who struggle. In S. J. Samuels & A. E. Farstrup (Eds.), *What research has to say about fluency instruction* (pp. 130–158). Newark, DE: International Reading Association.

Vacca, J. L., Vacca, R. T., Gove, M., Burkey, L. C., Lenhart, L. A., & McKeon, C. A. (2006). *Reading and learning to read* (6th ed.). Boston: Allyn and Bacon.

Wolf, M., & Katzir-Cohen, T. (2001). Reading fluency and its intervention. *Scientific Studies of Reading, 5,* 211–238.

Worthy, J., & Broaddus, K. (2001/2002). Fluency beyond the primary grades: From group performance to silent, independent reading. *The Reading Teacher, 55,* 334–343.

Yopp, R. H., & Yopp, H. K. (2003). Time with text. *The Reading Teacher, 57,* 284–287.

Yopp, H. K., & Yopp, R. H. (2000). Supporting phonemic awareness development in the classroom. *The Reading Teacher, 54,* 130–143.

Young, T. A., & Vardell, S. (1993). Weaving readers theatre and nonfiction into the curriculum. *The Reading Teacher, 46,* 396–406.

# Index